Design Thinking

This design focused series publishes books aimed at helping Designers, Design Researchers, Developers, and Storytellers understand what's happening on the leading edge of creativity. Today's designers are being asked to invent new paradigms and approaches every day – they need the freshest thinking and techniques. This series challenges creative minds to design bigger.

More information about this series at https://www.springer.com/series/15933

UX for XR

User Experience Design and Strategies for Immersive Technologies

Cornel Hillmann

Apress®

UX for XR: User Experience Design and Strategies for Immersive Technologies

Cornel Hillmann
Singapore

ISBN-13 (pbk): 978-1-4842-7019-6
https://doi.org/10.1007/978-1-4842-7020-2

ISBN-13 (electronic): 978-1-4842-7020-2

Managing Director, Apress Media LLC: Welmoed Spahr
Acquisitions Editor: Natalie Pao
Development Editor: James Markham
Coordinating Editor: Jessica Vakili

Distributed to the book trade worldwide by Springer Science+Business Media New York, 1 NY Plaza, New York, NY 10004. Phone 1-800-SPRINGER, fax (201) 348-4505, e-mail orders-ny@ springer-sbm.com, or visit www.springeronline.com. Apress Media, LLC is a California LLC and the sole member (owner) is Springer Science + Business Media Finance Inc (SSBM Finance Inc). SSBM Finance Inc is a **Delaware** corporation.

For information on translations, please e-mail booktranslations@springernature.com; for reprint, paperback, or audio rights, please e-mail bookpermissions@springernature.com.

Apress titles may be purchased in bulk for academic, corporate, or promotional use. eBook versions and licenses are also available for most titles. For more information, reference our Print and eBook Bulk Sales web page at http://www.apress.com/bulk-sales.

Any source code or other supplementary material referenced by the author in this book is available to readers on GitHub via the book's product page, located at www.apress.com/978-1-4842-7019-6. For more detailed information, please visit http://www.apress.com/source-code.

Printed on acid-free paper

For Audrey, LeNoir, LeMorbier, and LeInky

Table of Contents

About the Author

 **Cornel Hillmann** is a CG artist and XR designer with over 20 years of experience in the media and entertainment, advertising, and design industry. He's worked with brands including Panasonic, Jaguar, The Future Is Wild, the Singapore International Film Festival, Razor, and many others. Cornel started his career as an art director in Los Angeles after receiving his diploma in computer graphics. He founded CNT Media GmbH in Hamburg, Germany, and Emerging Entertainment Pte. Ltd. in Southeast Asia, before establishing studio.cgartist.com as a design studio in Singapore. Cornel has lectured master classes for immersive media postproduction and advanced 3D, VR, and media design courses at Limkokwing University and is the author of *Unreal for Mobile and Standalone VR* (Apress, 2019). Cornel spends most of his time using the Unreal engine for XR productions and enterprise visualizations.

During his spare time, you will find him in the VR multiplayer classic Dead and Buried II and occasionally in Population: One, Hyper Dash, and Altspace, unless jamming in his virtual synth studio, working on his personal passion projects, or writing software and creative tech reviews for his network partners.

About the Technical Reviewer

Tino Kuhn is a UX design lead and digital creative director, known to effortlessly combine creative storytelling and modern-day experience design with UX strategy and creative direction of digital marketing in different media and industry verticals. He has won several awards in creative advertising and digital marketing for his innovative ways in implementing impactful product experience on mobile platforms. His work includes UX design and strategy for such clients as Emirates, Vodafone, and Nando's, with a recent focus on education marketing and EdTech for innovative social platforms.

Tino established a new media design studio in his hometown Hamburg before moving to Melbourne, Australia, where he has continued his career as an early adopter of emerging technologies in the creative marketing space. He is currently working with Open Universities Australia, one of the biggest education and academic provider platforms in Australia. His passion for 360 video and VR gaming motivates him to develop a future gamified learning platform and a mental health app as a side gig.

Acknowledgments

The biggest thanks go out to my wife, Audrey, with her substantial support for my XR (extended reality) projects as a consultant, concept evaluator, tester, and critic.

An extra grateful thank you has to go to my technical reviewer, Tino, who spared no effort to deep dive into the subjects and challenges of this book project.

I also have to give my thanks to game design veteran Pascal Luban, for his in-depth discussion over UX (user experience) vs. game design and his insightful thoughts on the subject based on his long experience. My thanks go out to my cousin Wido Menhard, Executive Vice President of Digital Health at Siemens Healthineers, supporting my research of HoloLens AR applications in the medical field.

Special thanks to Mark Davies of Nexus Studios, Los Angeles, for his insights, time, and input as an industry professional from the perspective of a cutting-edge XR studio. A special shout-out to Sophia Prater whose innovative design system Object-Oriented UX (OOUX) might just be the missing link in XR design and UX design. A special thank you goes to the humancodable.org team, authors of the VR Advanced Framework for UE4, for discussing the role of frameworks and UX in XR. A special thanks to Singapore AR pioneers HelloHolo for letting me test the new HoloLens 2 when it first came out.

Thanks to the academic community in Singapore and the Unreal developer network, including the VR (virtual reality) association in Singapore and its helpful members.

And last but not least, thanks to the people who bought my previous book and inspired me to keep going with their appreciation and friendly encouragement.

Preface

This book is an exploration into the challenges and opportunities of designing for XR, an emerging space with a constantly changing landscape and almost daily breaking news of innovation. Therefore, it is an attempt to find a balance between landscape analysis and practical use case design evaluation. But other than pitching the dichotomy of academia vs. practice or hierarchical taxonomy vs. heuristic evaluation, the goal of this book is to capture all the elements that are driving the XR evolution forward, including history, ideas, platforms, as well as economic context and focus on the important concepts, very often lifted from toolsets or frameworks, that help designers, in their role as product designers, navigate the XR universe and give them a head start on the wider subject.

The book also reflects my journey as an XR designer coming from interaction and game design and adapting UX methodologies to XR projects that were previously governed by game design techniques, standards, and methods, typically centered around the game design document (GDD) as the product development hub. XR product design owes the majority of its tools and techniques to game design, which has evolved over the last decades from a tiny niche to the dominating entertainment industry that it is today. A development that could be repeated with XR products, if we get the user experience right.

I was first introduced to virtual reality by the late Timothy Leary, out of all people. Don't put down the book just yet. Leary was, at that point in the early to mid-1990s, way past his earlier role as the pied piper of the psychedelic generation; instead, he, in his senior years, advocated virtual reality as a vehicle for his bigger ideas. I met him at the very beginning of my career, while on my first real job as a designer in LA, introduced by a close friend. His enthusiastic techno utopian vision about the liberation of mankind through VR seemed wild and way over the top, to my job-focused mind at the time. Back then he wrote: "Electronic reality is more real than the physical world! This is a profound evolutionary leap. It can be compared to the jump from ocean to shoreline, when land and air suddenly become more real to the ex-fish than water!" (Timothy Leary, *Chaos & Cyberculture*, 1994, page 48). Even two years earlier, in 1992, at the age of 72, he explained in a press conference of the Travel and Tourism Research Association in Minneapolis that "Virtual reality will one day make business travel all but obsolete, since people will be able to come together electronically to create…telepresence" (a quote from an article in the *Baltimore Sun*, from June 16, 1992).

People at that time, including my youngster self, were reacting with skepticism: "Great ideas, but it's not going to happen in our lifetime."

Nevertheless, hanging out with such a counterculture icon taught me a lesson: Never underestimate the power of big ideas. As it turned out, he was right on a lot of his predictions that became a reality 20 years later. When I was able to get my hands on the DK1 (Development Kit 1) for the Oculus Rift in 2014, my mind was blown. Once I stepped into a life-scale 3D space that I had modeled and designed earlier and was able to move around in it using the DK1, I was more than sold. It was a life-changing moment to be able to live in your own virtual creation. The idea of being able to build your own reality echoing back conversations that took place 20 years earlier gave me more than nerd chills; it injected me with a new dose of purpose and vision.

UX design, on the other hand, was an acquired taste for me, after I first discovered it about a decade ago. Like an exotic fruit, it first tasted sweet and bitter at the same time and had to grow on me over time. Bitter, because it forced me to rethink a lot of ways in which I previously worked. Sweet, because I began to appreciate the elegance and depth of its systems and the advantages of a shared language that brings everyone together on the same page. Game design has a lot of similar components as UX design – user research, stakeholder interviews, prototyping, and focus group tests – but the UX design process is embedded into a whole canon of product design systems and philosophies that, navigating it under the general ideas of design thinking, makes it satisfying and results oriented, with the extraordinary success stories of the digital economy partly owed to it. Game design used to put less emphasis on user research and UX methods because the attitude was often "I'm not biased, I just happen to know what users want," but that is also partially due to the fact that the game industry is often a very different animal and, to a great degree, genre driven.

The mission of this book is to map the territory, take a snapshot of where we are in the XR department of the digital transformation process, lay out approaches to XR design problems, and give hints and pointers to problem-solving ideas. The two biggest groups this book approaches are, on one hand, XR game designers interested in adopting UX design principles and, on the other hand, UX designers coming from web and mobile design, ready to take on XR. Covering the two different angles means either party will find some information they already know. Game designers most likely understand the role of visual scripting for frameworks, while UX designers probably don't need an explanation of the double diamond. Nevertheless, it is important to cover both angles, because the mission of the book is to bring both of these loose ends together. The beauty of applying the UX design process to digital product design in the XR space means working with a winning formula that is proven to be successful. A special shout-out in this context is due to my technical reviewer, Tino Kuhn, whom I've been following for a long time, observing his inspiring career as a UX lead. Tino went well out his way to spend extra time and effort to evaluate the ideas of the book and guide the workshops that led to the practical examples, especially those covered in the last chapter. His extensive knowledge and experience as a workshopper for enterprise projects helped to keep the focus on the main goals.

The goals are to get people started in XR design, to give an overview over ideas, platforms, tools, concepts, and useful design systems and interaction patterns.

Looking back at how design patterns have evolved over this incarnation of VR, which started back in 2013 with the Oculus Rift on Kickstarter, gives an idea of how much has happened since.

During the early baby steps, when the Oculus Rift was launched in 2016, the buzzword was "presence," and the UX focus was on what not to do: Don't break immersion, don't make people sick, don't do anything unnatural if possible. Fast forward to 2021 and no one talks about "presence" anymore; instead, we keep using the term *immersion* in its place, because it is more useful in differentiating the context. The paranoia about immersion breaking actions and unnatural motion has been contained, because we understand it much better now and are instead starting to embrace the opposite by often endorsing superpowers.

The intention of this book is to be a primer on the subject, including the important contextual information. XR game designers will hopefully understand how UX thinking is beneficial to a production, while UX designers, coming from web and mobile design, will get a complete overview of where things are coming from and are headed toward and what techniques, tools, or platforms to use.

The book identifies prototyping as one of the main pain points for UX designers. The game engine–based process for fully functional and interactive prototypes is still a very complex and technical enterprise with a steep learning curve, or a "bag of hurt" as Steve Jobs would have said. But there is hope on the horizon, for example, the upcoming version of the XR design tool Tvori with basic interaction simulations. To be able to design in context using a spatial design app is ultimately the best long-term scenario for designers.

Finally, we should acknowledge that UX design for XR will only be mastered if one understands the secrets and wisdom of the *exit burrito*.

What is the *exit burrito*? Turns out, it's not your last meal before leaving this planet, but instead the way to end a game in the VR title *Job Simulator*. You have to grab a burrito from a suitcase and stuff it into your face with two bites to confirm your intentions to exit the game. The wisdom behind it is: The weirdest interactions can become surprisingly satisfying when paired meaningfully and playtested properly. The secret to unlocking XR creativity is: The idea of literal gestures triggering meaningful action opens the door to endless opportunities. How about literally kicking a can down the road in VR to extend playtime or to literally hold a stake in a VR meeting to identify a stakeholder, when raising hands? Well, this can get pretty silly, but at the same time fun and inspirational, and that is what XR is all about. It's playtime for the mind.

We are currently moving into a mature state of the industry, but the innovations are just getting started to hit big time. The VR-associated gaming platform Rec Room has become a unicorn, currently valued at US$ 1.25 billion, and a US Army deal has secured Microsoft a US$ 21.88 billion contract for the HoloLens. In the meantime, Snapchat, Niantic, and Apple are preparing the launch for their own AR glasses, while designers were recently provided with a Figma UI toolset for the HoloLens MRTK (Mixed Reality Toolkit). All these are signs that things are coming together and doors are opening to an XR future full of opportunities.

The Metaverse is on its way in, alongside technologies that will change our life. In the last part of the book, the topics blockchain and NFTs (nonfungible tokens) are discussed in an XR context. A very polarizing subject, due to the rise of cryptocurrencies, speculative excess, and bubble fears. But before generalizing Bitcoin & Co and the underlying future technology, I would say: Hold…or better yet *hodl*…your horses. Blockchain technology will be part of our future in one way or another, apart from how hyperactive financial markets deal with it. It may even be devoid of greed and possibly become minerless, free, feeless, regulated, and green or even help with climate change accountability – promising initiatives to accomplish that are on the way (including blockchainforclimate.org).

If this book inspires you to take it a step further and dive deeper into VR development using the Unreal game engine, I recommend you have a look at my first book, *Unreal for Mobile and Standalone VR* (Apress, 2019). The book covers all steps to create professional VR applications from scratch, using Blueprint visual scripting and efficient production pipeline techniques. It also includes two complete tutorials: a VR product presentation and a VR puzzle game.

Another resource worth mentioning is my own website, where I will be updating contextual information for this book, including updates on the Reality UX Lab project mentioned in Chapters 4 and 6. Please feel free to join the discussion and share your feedback and input at studio.cgartist.com.

—Cornel Hillmann

CHAPTER 1

Introduction

The extended reality (XR) era is here, and its rise will have an increasing visibility in the decade ahead of us. The 2020s is the beginning of a wider adoption of the next computing platform after years of experimentation and innovation.

The intention of this book is to give an overview of the opportunities in extended reality application for UX designers, as well as to evaluate the approaches and techniques of user experience (UX) design targeting virtual reality (VR) and augmented reality (AR) applications for XR developers and producers.

The reasons for that are obvious: UX design is a success story. The rise of UX design in the last decade is reflected in the overwhelming success of the mobile economy, which was to a large degree driven by the refining of UX standards, techniques, and tools for maximum efficiency and impact (Figure 1-1).

© Cornel Hillmann 2021
C. Hillmann, *UX for XR*, https://doi.org/10.1007/978-1-4842-7020-2_1

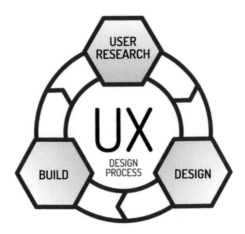

Figure 1-1. *The UX design process (image by C. Hillmann)*

UX design is now a well-oiled machine when it comes to web and mobile app development. It has been proven to work; it has been shown to create success stories and wealth in the digital economy. Over the last 10 years, we have seen the rise of a whole UX universe with conventions, industry bodies, training courses, literature, and a healthy demand in the job market. Even though the role of UX is constantly being refined and debated, it is here to stay, because it fulfills its promise to optimize the user experience, which in turn means to create successful digital products and to ensure user retention rates.

AR and VR applications, as part of an emerging XR industry, have had a mixed record when it comes to user retention numbers. Due to the constantly changing landscape of formats, technological breakthroughs, and software and hardware platforms, it has been difficult to establish a winning formula to attract a critical mass of satisfied users, with a number of notable exceptions.

Facing this situation, which as a whole is very typical for an emerging technology, makes it obvious that XR application development needs UX design and strategy more than ever. It is crucial for the success of an emerging industry to monitor user behavior and refine its key components based on that data.

The UX design approach that has worked so well for web and mobile applications is, to a great degree, transferable to XR application development, when it comes to its guiding principles. Nevertheless, when it comes to the practical application in the production process, it is faced with a number of obstacles due to technical and format hurdles.

The idea of this book is to identify what has been learned so far, regarding UX design for XR applications, and what areas still need to be refined in terms of UX standards while evaluating possible solutions for the inevitable pain points.

In this way, this book aims to help analyze UX practices for XR environments and review the techniques and tools for prototyping and designing XR user interactions. The objective is to approach the design for experiential state and spatial cognition, using established UX KPIs, while taking into account the social dynamics, emotional framework, and wider industry context.

1.1 Welcome to the Spatial Computing Era

Coined as "the next big thing" by Apple CEO Tim Cook on January 21, 2020, augmented reality will "pervade our entire lives" over the next 5–10 years. Virtual reality is already building momentum with the success of the Oculus Quest by Facebook, while AR devices such as the Magic Leap and Microsoft's HoloLens are building their technical and usability frameworks and community. The rise of XR technology is redefining how humans interact with digital content, and new possibilities are bringing a major shift in UX strategies and design to revolutionize human-computer interaction (HCI). While user experience design has risen to the center stage of organizations to build meaningful and relevant experiences for their users on digital devices with flat screens, a new era of spatial interaction is transforming the design space and its techniques around storytelling, interaction design, strategy, research, and information architecture.

Extending traditional digital platforms to the new frontier of XR requires taking into account what best practices, new concepts, and conventions have been established and what learnings can be brought forward from case studies involving industry leaders. Looking at practical examples from the field of handheld AR (HAR) breakthroughs, VR success stories, and experimental interaction concepts of pioneering XR platforms allows us to map out a framework of UX guidelines, thus closing in on opportunities and challenges that lie ahead. Even though the XR landscape is constantly changing, it holds a set of promises to the user that are long term and are unlikely to change as the technology matures (Figure 1-2).

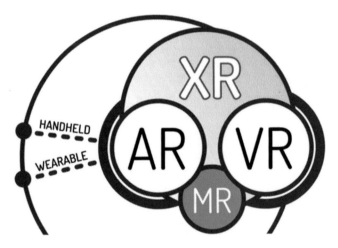

Figure 1-2. *Extended reality (XR) (image by C. Hillmann)*

The perspective of UX for XR is to focus on the user benefits, analyze what works best by having empathy for the user, and articulate solutions for design problems. While this mission is clear, it is very often the technical complexity and the novel prospects of the XR medium that carry an additional weight in the scope of work for UX XR design work. What it comes down to is the fact that a UX designer targeting XR applications does not have to be a coder, but does have to understand how the technology works and what implications design decisions have, when it comes to technical dependencies. Once the groundwork is done, a wide space of opportunities opens up. It is very often the excitement of pioneering design work that builds momentum in emerging technologies. The passion of UX designers inspired by the new opportunities in XR is fueling innovation, and these designers, by taking user agency, are making sure that these ideas work for the intended audience.

1.2 Mapping the Territory: UX

The general concept of user experience design has been around for centuries, and, in hindsight, it seems logical that it culminated in a flourishing design industry that is shaping the digital economy today.

But, while UX design for electronic devices and digital applications has been around since the 1990s, it only took center stage in the last decade. The overwhelming success of the iPhone and the rise of the digital economy centered around mobile devices, plus the need to unify the design for web and mobile applications for consistency, made UX design an unparalleled success story. Taking a user-centric design approach, applying research, and testing routines turned out to be the right approach for the digital economy. It was the driver behind most of the ecommerce shooting stars and the secret sauce that helped disruptive unicorns to capture the platform economy era.

But let's not forget that the remarkable rise of UX design is a fairly recent phenomenon. Before 2009, the UX designer job description was practically unknown in the job market. Although it existed in the context of HCI research and usability testing facilities with a few larger organizations, it was, in the end, Apple that radically committed to the UX concept as a core process for developing new products. As a result, it turned the company into the most valuable public company in the world, dominating every industry it took on. As design legend Don Norman, who joined Apple in the early 1990s, pointed out: UX entails all aspects of the user's interaction with the company, its services, and its products.

This very holistic design approach is today very often overshadowed by the typical work of UX designers. Not out of ignorance, but out of practical considerations. Most designers in the UX field working on apps and websites have no control over the devices their design solution is used on. Their work is focused on the digital product and its user interaction alone, while the device UX is of course handled by the hardware developer.

This situation has created the misleading conception that UX design is actually UI design for the most part. Job descriptions very often underline this notion by advertising for UX/UI designers. Once again, not by ignorance, but out of practical considerations. A lot of UX design for mobile and web applications is centered around UI interaction. Typical examples are ecommerce and booking apps, where the user flow is directly mirrored in the interaction with the UI. As a matter of fact, it is a very common misconception that UX design means the design side of front-end development only. But that may only be a distorted perception, because it just happened to be where most of the work was.

With the transition into the XR era, this is going to gradually change, and UX design will actually find its way back to its holistic roots of considering all aspects of the interaction between a design and its user, due to the fact that this interaction will entail a lot more than just a UI (Figure 1-3).

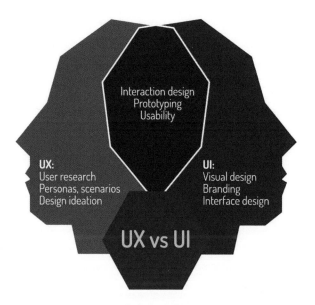

Figure 1-3. *UX vs. UI design (image by C. Hillmann)*

Spatial interaction, gestures, and speech are just a few of the new elements that will define the new paradigm. As a matter of fact, the X in UX, the experience factor, will weigh in on a new level and will refine what experience actually means in an XR context.

The term *experience* has been somewhat overused in the early wave of VR enthusiasm, when every company wanted one. Designing a VR experience instead of a VR app sounded more exciting and entailed a lot more promises of capturing the user's attention with immersive technologies.

Nevertheless, the frenzy of the early VR hype is way behind us, and the term *experience* is still a good and descriptive term for an XR app, as it expresses a user-centric interaction that entails more than a few finger swipes on a screen. It addresses multiple senses and has the potential to completely simulate the real world and the many ways a human interacts with it.

For UX designers, this is a whole new playing field with endless opportunities, but also a huge amount of problems to solve (Figure 1-4).

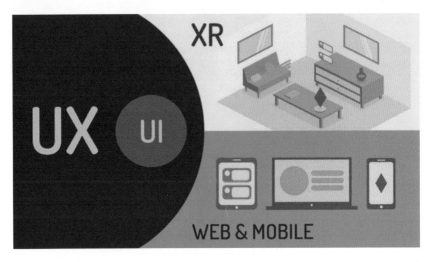

Figure 1-4. *UX and UI design for spatial computing vs. mobile and web (image by C. Hillmann)*

Think about it. For the longest time, one of the biggest headaches for UX/UI designers pushing out prototypes in the mobile and web space has been responsive designs: making user interaction consistent across various screen formats and sizes and resolutions, using fluid grids, anchors, responsive breakpoints, and device templates. Tools such as Sketch, Adobe XD, and Figma, to name a few, have been helpful in prototyping designs that were very close to the actual final product on various devices.

The problem of responsive design could potentially be a much tougher nut to crack in the XR space, if you are aiming to have consistency between AR handheld devices, such as tablets and AR wearables as AR glasses, based on the same content. Both device categories interact with the same spatial environment, but the user interacts with the content in dramatically different ways. Tapping a spatial AR object on a tablet could fill the majority of the screen space with a contextual UI, but wearing

AR glasses viewing the same space in stereoscopic 3D would have a devastating effect, if an activated UI floats close to the user's eyes, blocking their field of view (FoV).

UX designers for web and mobile apps had to deal mostly with flat rectangles of different sizes and orientations, horizontal and vertical. Wearable AR with an endless screen and a spatial component adds a design challenge to UX conventions.

UX design for web and mobile applications has so far lived in framed rectangles: the horizontal rectangle for the standard monitor and the vertical rectangle for the mobile phone, plus the mix of both for the rest of mobile devices, including tablets, as experienced through responsive design. The limitation of a flat rectangular design space is a convenience for designers. It allows the focus on a framed flat surface without spatial dependencies. The rectangular screen space is the successor of the book page without the responsive and interactive elements and can therefore draw from thousands of years of history of designing and organizing a rectangular surface space to appeal to a user who is already very familiar with it.

The XR space completely breaks away from this tradition and consistency. On one side, it is more at home in the realms of simulation technology, but on the other side also closer to the immersive worlds of theater, magic, and storytelling. But the arch that really connects both the non-XR and the XR user experience design is the high-concept approach of solving design problems by learning about the user's needs, building prototypes, and testing them until they work as intended.

1.3 Mapping the Territory: XR

UX design is very often associated with marketing and CX (the customer experience) as an umbrella category, with strong links to advertising, graphic design, and Apple computers. Sketch, the UX application of choice for designers for the longest time before Figma took over, is only available on Apple devices, and, very often, typical UX designers have a background in graphic, screen, or UI design.

The XR world is inherently a bit of a different animal here. Its home is originally the world of 3D and game engines (and is therefore more Windows oriented). The fact that most XR applications are produced with game engines, like Unity or Unreal, brings them also closer to the game development community. Some XR applications have been games, but even in the case of an EdTech or enterprise XR project, the resources, talent, pipeline, and production technique would be based on game development standards (Figure 1-5).

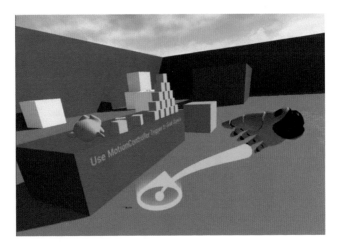

Figure 1-5. *VR prototyping using an Unreal engine template*

Games have used and still use UX as part of the design process that is very often focused on UI interaction. UX design and game design have to some degree merged happily with the rise of mobile games in the last decade, but the focus of UX in game design remains on the UI, up to today (UX game design jobs are most often advertised as UX/UI positions, indicating a UI focus).

A legitimate question would be: How were games designed without UX design techniques based on user flows and storytelling?

The answer is that game design has always covered to a great degree what UX design does, when it comes to the more holistic tasks beyond UI interaction. User flows and storytelling are traditionally part of the game design document (GDD) that is the very foundation of every game production. The GDD describes in detail what the user is expected to do at any point in the game, how the game mechanics play out, and what components are part of the production. Part of that is also prototyping, usability testing, and game testing, including focus group tests.

Considering these facts, one would wonder, why would an XR production based on game development standards need UX at all?

The answer to that question is that game development standards are good for games, but for anything else, non-game XR apps, such as enterprise, B2B, MedTech, EdTech, and so forth, basic game design approaches fall short of understanding the user's needs. Games are really a special case in XR development, where the designer often knows their audience really well. Game designers usually know their audience better than UX designers, due to the nature of the game industry and its distinct genres and iterative game mechanics. UX designers, for web and mobile apps, very often have no idea about their users. That's why a strong focus is on acquiring knowledge about the user, creating personas and user journeys. UX design has also had a much stronger focus on conversion as part of the complete user journey, due to its closer ties to ecommerce, marketing, and advertising—think of booking apps, for example. Game designers, on the other hand, know their genre audience better and have a heads-up on what game mechanics are popular with the user base and what pitfalls to avoid. Plus, gamers are very vocal, proactive, visible, and thus easier to profile. Most games are built on the foundation of already established and popular game mechanics and iterate in genre variations and graphics style, in a familiar spectrum of genres, with a typical profile of the genre's user.

UX design becomes very important when designing an XR application that is not primarily for a known user base of genre gamers, where the audience and the content is a blank canvas.

This is where the UX design approach becomes important: the process of understanding the user, understanding the motives of using the application, through targeting personas and scenarios, making storytelling and user flow work for them and testing the results (Figure 1-6).

Figure 1-6. *XR prototype example by Microsoft Maquette*

For example, think about the UX design for an XR MedTech app that is targeting healthcare professionals working in hospitals. To make an XR application work for a user base that is busy with a lot of other responsibilities, the UX design process is key in making the concept work in an area where we have a lot of unknowns.

UX design and UX research routines have proven themselves to tackle this very problem: getting into the shoes of the user and finding solutions for user problems through iterative prototyping.

Next to solving design problems, UX design has another advantage: Due to its enormous success in the digital economy and based on the fact that it is the driving force behind most of the ecommerce unicorns (think Uber, AirBnB, etc.), the UX design process is building trust among the project stakeholders. People do understand that UX is important and crucial for a digital product to succeed. The UX design process has a pretty impressive track record. There are good reasons to use UX methodologies on emerging technology with audiences who may be unfamiliar with its novel possibilities. For UX designers, that means it is important to understand all the components and pitfalls of the wider XR field, in order to deliver design solutions on a high-concept level, without needing to touch any code.

1.4 Merging the UX and the XR Universe

It may be important to be sensible toward a possible culture clash between the UX and the XR world. As mentioned in the previous paragraph, XR is by its roots at home in the game development world, while UX design, the way it is most visible in the job market, has been associated with marketing and SaaS (Software as a Service) applications. This fact is also reflected in communication and specifically in language and terminology.

For example, a UX designer may speak of establishing a "customer journey map," while a game designer could speak about a "game progression chart," but both essentially mean a similar thing. It may be important for both perspectives to open up and understand each other's technical language and jargon, to better cooperate to the benefit of team play.

The successful merger between the player-centric UX approach and the established game developer toolset has been shown to work wonders with mobile games, where it was first established during its rise within the last decade. The UX approach gives game design an edge by giving guidance and bringing in the perspective of user behaviors and perceptions and thus bringing essential value to the development of a digital product. A fact that has been proven with a number of XR success stories that will be the blueprint for the XR UX going forward.

1.5 Crisis As an Accelerator

When Tim Cook announced the XR decade in early 2020, no one anticipated the worldwide pandemic and its devastating effects on human lives and the economy. Once the scope of destruction became obvious, it also became clear that a number of gradual changes will play out over the next decade in how humans interact, cooperate, and do business, facing a world where physical interaction may be unsafe or unwise. Governments have been pushing digital transformation efforts to help the economy meet these challenges, and XR technologies are at the forefront of these endeavors.

In this sense, the pandemic crisis has been an accelerator for the wider XR industry. Online conferencing including social VR numbers is up, and a new wave of virtual meetup solutions is helping businesses work around the new normal without physical conferences and meetings (Figure 1-7).

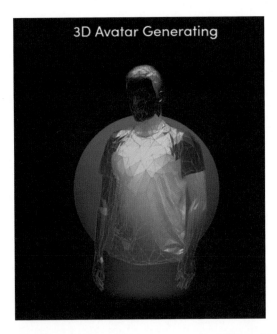

Figure 1-7. *Generating a Spatial.io avatar for VR online collaboration*

While these solutions were triggered by short-term needs, they will have long-lasting effects, as organizations and businesses, as well as consumers, gradually appreciate the convenience and benefits of XR when it comes to online social interaction and teamwork.

The pandemic crisis will go down in history as a turning point for XR. While economic challenges are undeniably present for the economy as a whole, it is the promise of XR to overcome limitations of the physical world and open up a future where people can meet, shop, and cooperate in a virtual environment.

No matter how big the challenges of the present are, the drive for a digital future is bigger than ever, while XR developers and UX designers are helping to make it happen. A flourishing virtual space will pull the physical world, or "meatspace" in classic VR jargon, with it, to the benefit of all.

1.6 Summary

This chapter looked at the big picture of emerging XR technologies and their implications for UX design. It evaluated the overlapping disciplines of UX design and game design and the challenges for UX designers to apply the same successful methods in VR and AR that made UX design a booming industry in the mobile era. Finally, it reviewed how the pandemic of 2020 made a great push for the digital transformation of society, accelerating the use of XR, to create safer and future-proof workspaces, benefiting other areas of the economy and bringing new opportunities to UX designers.

CHAPTER 2

The History and Future of XR

2.1 Introduction

This chapter will look at the big picture of the XR industry and what factors in its development are, foremost, relevant to UX design. This overview entails snapshots of the history of VR and AR, the elements that drive an XR experience, and the ecology of devices, technologies, use cases, as well as usability issues that frequently come up. The chapter will look at macro trends and future outlook behind spatial computing and the backstory of gamification and how it relates to the success story of UX design and XR in the digital economy.

2.2 XR: From Early Experiments to the Fourth Transformation

When the final version of the Oculus Quest standalone VR headset started shipping to consumers on May 21, 2019, numerous industry observers were speaking of the "iPhone moment" for VR. The headset was widely regarded as the first true consumer-friendly VR solution, the same way as the iPhone was the first true user-friendly smartphone when introduced in

© Cornel Hillmann 2021
C. Hillmann, *UX for XR*, https://doi.org/10.1007/978-1-4842-7020-2_2

2007, leaving in its wake all the numerous smartphone attempts that had frustrated and confused users with difficult-to-use interfaces and menus. The Quest was using the full potential of six degrees of freedom (6DOF) motion tracking in a package that was easy to set up and use without having to connect to a computer (Figure 2-1).

Figure 2-1. *Facebook's Oculus Quest 1 (image by C. Hillmann)*

Oculus under the new owner, Facebook, made sure that this new product line would be as polished as it could possibly be while keeping the price under the affordable $400 price point, comparable to traditional gaming consoles.

It is no surprise that Facebook, a company that owes part of its global success to its ongoing dedication to HCI and UX research, put such a strong emphasis on the user experience of not only software but also hardware, branding, and onboarding. From the slick device aesthetics to the well-laid-out onboarding using the polished "first steps—introduction to VR" app and the ease of creating the guardian play area, the product launch had all the ingredients of a historic milestone device, especially from a UX perspective. Defining the device category "standalone 6DOF HMD," the Quest succeeded in areas where previous variations of VR headsets were struggling. The follow-up model Quest 2 turned out to be an even bigger success, surpassing the monthly active people of the original Quest in only 7 weeks.

2.2.1 UX Before Oculus VR

The Facebook acquisition of Oculus was widely criticized by the VR community, which regarded the move as a betrayal of the independent spirit that the original Oculus crowdfunding campaign on Kickstarter in 2012 had ignited. Other voices pointed out that synergies between the extensive resources of the social media giant and the emerging VR brand would have a positive impact on the overall XR industry and its stride to become mainstream.

During the history of VR before 2012, UX design and research had not played a major role, due to the fact that developers were struggling with the limitations of the technology. Bulky hardware, limited processing power, low resolution, and underperforming frame rates were the foremost and biggest hurdles to a user-friendly experience. The failure of the first consumer VR wave in the 1990s did happen for the reason that the technology was not at a state that made a comfortable and meaningful user experience possible. Driven by the high expectations that iconic and pop culture–defining movies such as *Tron* (1982) and *The Lawnmower Man* (1992) evoked in the general public, the first attempts in early VR failed miserably. Arcade companies such as Virtuality, and VR gaming gear such as Nintendo's Virtual Boy, relied more on a novelty factor instead of providing actual, long-lasting entertainment value for the user.

Nevertheless, VR technology survived between the mid-1990s and 2012, mostly in research labs and with dedicated enterprise and education-oriented companies as in the case of Eon Reality, focusing on specific niche segments where VR actually worked and allowed for HCI usability research advances. It is noteworthy though that some of the most important interaction models such as hand gesture input were established as early as in 1982 by Thomas Zimmerman and VR pioneer Jaron Lanier. History shows that early groundbreaking concepts needed sufficient processing power and UX research to finally become usable.

2.2.2 The Timeline of UX for AR Devices

Looking at the history of AR, the timeline of progress, adoption, and UX breakthroughs seems to be more linear compared to VR, due to the fact that simple AR applications have an inherently lower entry bar when it comes to computing power requirements. Due to the fact that the area of useful application is, at first, much wider, when considering low-level industrial HUDs (head-up displays) and handheld AR assistant devices, on top of casual games and AR overlays as in Snapchat and other social media applications, AR became part of everyday life much earlier than VR.

The first historic breakthrough success for AR was without question the release of the mobile app Pokemon Go. The handheld AR game had reached 60 million active users by June 2017 and 1 billion downloads by 2019. Numbers never before seen in the context of a dedicated AR application, but also partly owed to the established and strong intellectual property owned by Nintendo, in addition to the innovative use of geo-tracking. No other handheld AR app had since been able to get anywhere close to these numbers, but it gave the general public an idea of the potential that AR has. AR developers were in the meantime given the opportunity to join the next evolutionary step into spatial computing: an immersive, stereoscopic, and interactive AR world pioneered by Microsoft with the HoloLens and the Magic Leap 1, by start-up Magic Leap, Inc., founded as early as 2010.

It was two decades earlier when the term *augmented reality* was credited to Boeing researcher Thomas P. Caudell in 1990, after the idea was first introduced by Ivan Sutherland in 1968. The first usable prototypes of wearable AR systems, such as the Battlefield Augmented Reality System (BARS) by the US Naval Research Laboratory, made their way

to specialized applications in 1999. Between the 1990s and the modern
mobile computing era, AR evolved from an experimental interactive tool
for specialized industrial and military applications to a technology that
gradually became ready for the wider consumer market. The rise of UX in
the 2010s and the growing availability of capable mobile phone cameras
finally opened the door to a wider commercial use for consumers, mostly
with handheld applications, to assist with often playful and experimental
information layers to explain products and services using AR pop-ups
triggered by embedded markers.

2.2.3 The Decade That Defined XR

One could say that the modern area of XR was defined in the decade
between 2010 and 2020. These 10 years saw the iterations of VR headsets,
from mobile phone–based Google Cardboard variations to high-end
enterprise solutions, driven foremost by HTC Vive and Oculus and the
evolution of handheld AR with the two main developer frameworks, ARKit
by Apple and ARCore by Google, plus the pioneering HMDs Magic Leap
and Microsoft's HoloLens.

The result of these developments, which were to a great degree niche
solutions and experimental in nature, was finally coming to a stage at
the end of the decade, where mobile computing power and software
breakthroughs allowed for a polished experience, opening the door to the
wider consumer market in the decade to follow.

2.2.4 Behind the Scenes of Industry 4.0

The backdrop of this development was a major transformation of the
economy, very often labeled Industry 4.0: the digitization of manufacturing
by data-driven, smart, decentralized systems, using among others artificial
intelligence (AI), Internet of Things (IoT), as well as XR solutions, to
optimize efficiency in the next chapter of industrial production.

The term *Industry 4.0* is very often referenced in popular concepts, such as the *fourth digital transformation*, describing a fundamental shift in consumer environments enabled by spatial computing. A transformation that not only affects businesses and consumers but also finds its way into civil engineering and GovTech, by improving services through data collection and process optimization for anything between the smart home and the smart city. The vision: better management of resources, in addition to better decision-making processes through real-time data transparency, enabling better services and consequently a better quality of life for all. The home and the city as a technology platform that interfaces with XR communication, using human-oriented computing, has been the projected long arch into the future.

The experimental XR decade of the 2010s was in many aspects the breeding ground for the breakthroughs that are expected to play out over the coming decade. It is widely expected that the new era will be dominated by spatial computing and wearable devices, driven by contextualized AI interfaces in XR. Mobile phones as the main drivers for growth and innovation will most likely become less relevant over time.

2.2.5 UX As a Market Maker for XR Applications

As previously noted, the 2010s also saw the rise of UX design as a crucial success factor for digital products. UX design and research has entered a phase of maturity and importance to the point that the contemporary UX design process is, without doubt, a major driver of consumer adoption and growth in the digital economy.

The spatial computing era and its new generation of XR devices will, to a great degree, rely on the power of UX design to succeed, as UX design and research is expected to be the key activator of this new era ahead. The challenge that lies ahead is to bring the wide field of technologies, formats, and interaction options that XR offers under the UX umbrella, in a way that the design solutions can be communicated between stakeholders.

Efforts in this direction have so far been successful on an individual device basis. It is of course easier to design within the limitations of a device such as a handheld tablet or a standalone VR headset than to develop a concept for the entire line of XR device categories, which may greatly differ in their individual technical capabilities.

Nevertheless, a number of important areas for UX principles are device independent and cover the entire spectrum of XR applications.

2.2.6 The Elements of XR Design

Even though XR devices can differ to a great degree, starting from handheld AR to standalone VR, there are a number of core elements that concern all UX approaches in XR. The most important areas are

a) Comfort and safety

b) Interaction (affordance, signifiers, feedback)

c) Environment and spatial components

d) Sensory input (visual, audio, haptics)

e) Engagement (storytelling, gamification)

f) Constraints

g) Inclusion, diversity, and accessibility

Comfort and safety:

Comfort and safety is, without doubt, one of the most important areas for UX design in XR. It has for the longest time been a massive problem throughout the history of XR, on both the software and the hardware side. Early VR headsets were basically prototypes and tech demos, where user comfort was not the priority. Even with the latest generation of HDMs, the problem persists, and the technology is often rejected by consumers due to comfort issues. It is a problem that will continually get better over time.

Nevertheless, UX designers need to have an awareness of the situation and assist with onboarding in the best possible way. Safety issues should not be underestimated, as users often attempt rapid movements and underestimate distances when wearing a headset. Reddit user groups are full of photos with injuries and appliance damages, as a result from gaming sessions that went out of control. The role of UX onboarding is, more than anywhere else, to guide the user through XR safety concerns and encourage, for example, reasonable distances and minimum play area reminders.

Interaction:

Interaction covers the specific UI/UX challenges in XR. The concern here is to communicate to the user how items can be interacted with. Questions include "Is an item usable?", "How do I use it?", "Am I doing the right thing?", "How do I get from point A to point B?", and "What locomotion options do I have?" It is important to look at the different signifier options in XR to make affordance as defined by Don Norman in "the design of everyday things" visible. An affordance is by that definition what an object can do, and a signifier helps to clarify that. A simple example would be a text pop-up over a drawer that reads "Open me."

Environment and spatial components:

Environment and spatial components play an important role in AR, when it comes to context, as the digital overlay is meant to interact with the actual environment that is always part of the experience. In VR, the environment plays a slightly different but still important role for UX design. Questions concerning play area, seated vs. standing, and orientation assistance touch on some of the most fundamental design considerations for the application, when it comes to the environment. The artificial environment is the core driver of the user experience, and design decisions regarding its spatial nature determine its storytelling nature. Spatial storytelling helps as the most important ingredient for the nonlinear approach of exploring a space with directional action.

Sensory input:

Sensory input options open up a rich toolbox of directing and orchestrating a user's experience through visual clues, audio navigation, as well as haptic feedback using the motion controllers. Spatial audio events, for example, can bring the user's attention to a specific hotspot by giving an incentive to turn around and refocus the field of view. Peripheral awareness with sound design can provide interactive context, and sound cues may help with navigating the user. Visual feedback based on gaze, such as highlighted objects at the center of the field of view or the controller's selection ray, may assist in completing tasks. Haptic controller feedback through vibration is often used as a call for action, for example, when an overlap event requires user action. While the interactive sensory input is the most obvious field for UX design, there is also the underlying visual design structure that touches questions beyond user interaction, such as fundamental audio-visual communication concepts, design systems, and style decisions.

Engagement:

Persistent user engagement is the result of successful UX design. For a digital XR product, that means guiding the user, eliminating the friction, giving incentives, and paving the way for satisfying and meaningful user experience, as a result of testing and prototyping, considering all spatial and sensory components. Storytelling and gamification play a big role to accomplish these goals. Both help to direct the user, provide goals, and play a crucial role in immersive environments, through an unfolding spatial narrative and the embedded feedback to keep going. "What am I supposed to do here?", "Am I facing the right way?", "What should I do next?", and "Is the task already finished?" are typical questions first-time XR users express. UX design for engagement in XR is crucial, because users are often disoriented, confused, or unclear about the objective of the product. The reason is often a lack of familiarity and routine with the technology. This problem can be addressed by monitoring user engagement during prototyping and user testing and by improving the results through incentives, adding and tweaking storytelling and gamification components.

Constraints:

To design, impose, and manage constraints is an important technique in spatial XR design. The idea is to manage the user's options, restrict unnecessary or harmful actions, and help with discoverability and feedback within the XR space. The most visible example is the guardian area that needs to be set up to restrict the VR play space. It is an effective way, and an industry standard, to constrain user movement with visual cues to prevent damage and injuries. Other areas to use constraints include fenced-off no-go terrains, axis restrictions on objects, and field-of-view limits to direct attention or avoid motion sickness. By disabling specific locomotion abilities, restricting access to areas, and limiting object interactions, constraints help the designer to direct the user experience. UX design for AR can be challenging as the natural constraints of the user's individual environment are unique in each case. Typically, it requires a flexible spatial design concept that takes the possible individual constraints of each user's environment into account.

Inclusion, diversity, and accessibility:

Inclusion, diversity, and accessibility are particularly important for the user. Wherever possible, one should consider the user's situation, their physical or mental abilities, cultural and ethnic backgrounds, and the sociological impact of the design—for example, encouraging diversity with engaging programming that counterbalances stereotypes or promoting inclusion by allowing a one-handed controller option in an XR application, for a user who has injuries or disabilities in one hand or arm.

Looking at these focus areas for XR design makes it possible to find common UX design rules that apply to both AR and VR. At its core, these rules are not permanently fixed, but instead constantly updated according to the latest result of experimentation and design experiences, as well as success stories and research data that developers and UX designers contribute to the XR communities.

Nevertheless, the questions always evolve around "What are the best ways to navigate through a space?", "What are the best ways to optimize the immersive nature of XR?", "How to design object interaction and discoverability in a spatial environment?", "What practices are most effective for a persistent and satisfying XR experience?", and "What are the pitfalls that break the user flow and presence in a digital XR product?"

2.2.7 XR: The Subculture Context

When considering the importance of cultural context in XR, we often evaluate how the user is affected by the cultural dimension of the design and how it influences the user's decision making, through familiarities and cultural background. Using established UX techniques such as personas and scenarios in user testing helps to understand cognitive bias and to apprehend the user's desires when interacting with the product.

One aspect that interacts with the perception of a digital XR product is the cultural history and pop culture context of the technology itself. A fact that can play a role in the user's expectation and perception of an XR design. Depending on the target audience, an XR designer can tap into that to the advantage of the experience.

VR has had a long history as a subculture in a science fiction and gaming context. Game culture has played an increasingly important role in pop culture. For example, the concept of gamer bait, a term that defines the idea of attracting users using game aesthetics in advertising, is one of the marketing reverberations of this trend. VR culture can be seen as a part of the gaming subculture with its own distinct retrofuturism style. For that reason, it is a good idea to understand the historical and cultural context of VR that is still relevant today. Examples are terminology, visual references, and XR concepts that have their origin in sci-fi pop culture, such as the Metaverse from Neal Stephenson's novel *Snow Crash* and the Oasis in Ernest Cline's novel *Ready Player One*, as another name for a multiplayer VR cloud.

Visual references include classic 1980s sci-fi design, as neon glow on wireframe surface edges from vintage sci-fi classics such as *Tron* and floating HUDs from the Spielberg adaptation of *Ready Player One* in 2018. Very often, ironic references to the first generation of VR designs in the late 1980s and early 1990s are used in a tongue-in-cheek way, as a homage and a hipster statement.

These references are building a framework of expectation and subculture reference, often considered "nerd culture" with a backdrop of Internet memes and related niche music genres from Vaporwave to Synthwave, referencing the often cheesy, but today considered stylish, dreamworlds of 1980s futurism.

VR was, in its early days in the late 1980s and early 1990s, a staple of counterculture iconography, very often seen in the context of early hacker and cyberpunk subculture, going back to publications such as the magazines *Mondo 2000* in 1989 and *Reality Hackers* in 1988. In the spirit of that time, personal liberation, consciousness expansion, and the transformation of culture through an altered reality were the projected endgame of the technology.

Not surprisingly, a counterculture icon at that time, the late Timothy Leary, was advocating VR as the successor to the psychedelic movement. The early subculture enthusiasm for the potential of VR and its transformation of culture over time is well documented through the work of VR pioneer Jaron Lanier, who remains one of the most influential writers on the topic.

XR, its subculture history, sci-fi media context, role in design, and related futurist thinking, is very often mapped within the philosophical terrain of transhumanism. Often considered a controversial or highly debated topic, transhumanism covers a wide field of speculative positions regarding the relationship between human beings and technology and how that relationship will evolve in the future. Even though there are numerous branches of transhumanist thinking, the common denominator is the idea that technology will transform the human condition and greatly expand its potential. In this context, XR technology is adding "superpowers" to the limited human senses and physical abilities.

From the perspective of the XR designer, it makes sense to have a good understanding of the XR universe in terms of history, subculture, and design culture, to be able to tap into these resources, when it comes to conceptualizing a consumer product that may benefit from referencing this cultural framework.

2.2.8 UX Design for Life 4.0

Whenever a term with the appendix 4.0 appears in the context of future computing, it can be assumed that it is a reference to the term *Industry 4.0*, as previously noted. The concept that originated through a German government initiative in 2011 and advocated the digitization of manufacturing, including interconnected and decentralized smart technologies to automate and improve the industrial manufacturing process. 4.0 refers to the industrial eras in history: 1.0, the transition from manual labor to machines; 2.0, the change to mass production and electricity; 3.0, the introduction of automation, electronics, and computers; and, finally, the rise of 4.0, smart networked technologies, cloud computing, big data, IoT, AI, and XR, as part of a macro trend to disrupt and innovate the economy at large.

In contrast to the Industry 4.0 concept, there is also the concept of the fourth digital transformation of consumer behavior based on technological innovation, but tied into a different timeline (Figure 2-2).

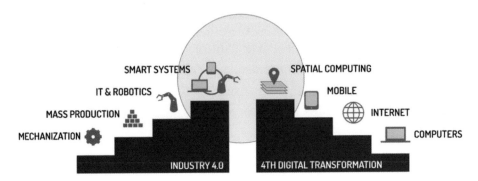

Figure 2-2. *Industry 4.0 and the fourth transformation (image by C. Hillmann)*

At the current state on this timeline, occasionally called Life 4.0, the consumer world is transforming to a world driven entirely by data-driven, digital interaction, at home and at work. A transformation that will eventually affect all aspects of life, where virtual meetings and smart home appliances seamlessly interact with XR devices. The evolutionary steps on this timeline up to now included the following stages in history: (1) the introduction of the personal computers, (2) the Internet, (3) mobile computing and finally the transformation that is currently on the way, and (4) wearable spatial computing, smart and cloud enabled.

2.2.9 XR as a UX-Driven Marketing Paradise?

It is no surprise that marketing strategists get excited over the possibilities of XR in this new era. The prospects of monitoring consumer behaviors, tracking locations, personal preferences, and allowing to overlay the spatial discovery process in XR with contextual and personalized marketing offers, in worst-case, spatial pop-up ads, are a dream come true for ecommerce strategists, eager to take advantage of the upcoming experience economy. The opportunities to bring businesses and customers together through a cloud-enabled XR layer, and to customize sales messages based on location, gaze, and personal preference, are enormous. A new ecosystem with AR billboards and valuable virtual real estate is awaiting the first platform to establish consumer traction in this space.

But before getting too excited about XR-based ecommerce, we should also consider that there are skeptical voices, expressing concerns about privacy, among others. The policy discussion in the context of consumer privacy vs. the big tech FAANG companies (Facebook, Amazon, Apple, Netflix, Google) has introduced the political term *surveillance capitalism*, an expression that describes the skepticism, anxiety, and critical views on emerging technologies in the context of the global platform economy.

The socioeconomic environment has an influence over how a user perceives a product, and if data security and privacy are increasingly major concerns, then UX designers have the opportunity and responsibility to address and communicate the product's policies in this regard. The goal is to deliver an experience that includes transparency on data collection and information in which context data is collected and for what purpose personal data will be used, if permitted.

2.2.10 UX for XR in EdTech, MedTech, and Beyond

XR-based ecommerce, product showcases and tryouts, guides, entertainment, and games are the most visible XR areas. Growth has picked up in all these segments, and investment analysts expect the biggest push to come once the leading tech companies present their AR wearables targeting consumers at a moderate price point.

Areas that are not quite as visible, but nevertheless have shown respectable results in efficiency and problem solving, are XR solutions in EdTech, MedTech, and corporate training.

A recent study by PwC on training and education in VR concluded that VR is an effective way to not only teach job skills but also soft skills such as leadership, resilience, and change management. The study concluded that VR participants were able to learn four times faster, with 3.5 times higher emotional connection while being 2.5 times more confident and four times more focused.

Education is one of the biggest beneficiaries of XR, where both AR and VR show their unique strength. While AR is able to give a contextual overlay as a learning aid, the unique strength of VR is to be able to spread out complex information in a space not limited by monitor size. The ability to use an entire 360-degree stereoscopic environment to organize, present, and manage learning content, plus the shielded focus, makes it an almost ideal candidate for efficiency and cost-effectiveness at scale.

MedTech is another area where XR applications have been able to gain a foothold with innovative approaches and proven results. From telemedicine to training for medical staff and surgical training up to better patient communication, the field of XR in medical applications is rapidly growing in relevance to provide better and more efficient services.

One example is the Cinematic Reality application for the Microsoft HoloLens 2 by Siemens Healthineers. The application is able to render voxel data from CT and MRI scans with a Monte Carlo path tracer and HDR lighting in real time at 60 fps, using a histogram transfer function. The result is a stereoscopic and interactive hologram of the scanned body part in realistic colors and shading that allows the surgeon to explore possible solutions for a difficult operation with a HoloLens headset. It also makes patient communication easier and helps to transfer information between radiology and clinical staff.

Cinematic Reality for the HoloLens by Siemens Healthineers is a very good example of how XR technology gives a better overview over a complex set of data and thus assists in better and faster decision making.

The advances of XR in MedTech and EdTech are not as headline grabbing as the billion Pokemon Go downloads, but they can be seen in a larger context of civic XR applications, where, as in the case of GovTech, UX design is critically important for its role in capacity building.

The XR era in the coming decade and beyond will most likely be driven by the huge ecosystem of start-ups, tech investors, innovators, and content creators that have been betting on the commercial breakthrough of XR applications, based on XR devices, that are affordable and capable enough to go mainstream.

But it is important to keep in mind that outside of the commercial limelight is a less visible transformation using XR applications in applied sciences for humanity. These areas include innovation in urban solutions, health technologies, and renewable energy. XR is bringing better analytics, communication, and problem-solving tools to these essential growth areas, and UX designers are key in helping to turn these complex ideas into comprehensible and intuitive user experiences. Considering the wide field of XR devices and applications, it is apparent that the most visible advances in recent years fall into the area of VR.

2.3 VR: A Roller-Coaster Ride into the Future

VR has been on a bumpy ride, even in its great second wave. If there is one idea that represents the uneven history, volatile emotions, and the often gimmicky nature of VR demos, then it must be the image of the roller coaster. Not only was a virtual roller coaster one of the earliest applications for the first Oculus development kit and therefore the introduction to VR for most early enthusiasts but the roller coaster also represents, in a sues around VR simulation sickness and the ups and downs of enthusiasm and disappointment for its role as a future key technology within the XR universe. For that reason, it is interesting to examine what role UX had played in the complicated recent history of VR.

2.3.1 When UX Thinking Was Injected into VR: The Epic Story of Oculus

After the first VR consumer hype in the 1990s had crashed miserably, due to underpowered technology, unrealistic expectations, and design principles that put novelty before usability, as mentioned earlier, it took the idea another two decades to take another shot at the broader market.

While, in the meantime, NASA research labs were evaluating VR for space applications behind closed doors and niche engineering applications such as Virtools were used for prototyping industrial VR simulations, it was not until 2012 when modding enthusiast and headset collector Palmer Luckey and developer legend John Carmack collaborated on a VR HMD prototype that had a significantly larger field of view than anything else at that time. The first development kit became the most successful kick-starter project of all times and led to the 2 billion Facebook buyout in 2014, an event that triggered the most recent VR hype. The enthusiasm tapered off a few years later, as many early investors in VR-related start-ups were disappointed by the lack of scale. Despite that, these events triggered the new era of VR, and eventually long-term investors returned, impressed by the commitment of a dedicated global VR community.

Palmer Luckey was the evangelist for a new generation of affordable VR for gamers and consumers. Despite being a polarizing figure for the political views he later expressed, he has to be credited with bringing the technology to the consumer and with that a UX push to make the latest VR technology enjoyable outside of research and industrial use.

Early Oculus concepts by Palmer and Carmack set the broader vision: next to a wider field of view, motion-tracked controllers, audio features, and support by the major game engines, which in turn opened the door for developers to experiment with UX ideas. Palmer's dedication gave a push to eras that were previously overlooked, as, due to failure in the 1990s and its niche in research, the technology was not considered usable for consumer entertainment and gaming.

The early years of Oculus VR between 2010 and 2013 were, coincidentally, also the years when UX design emerged as a powerful force, shaping the digital economy in its own terms. Early discussions among UX professionals noted the new challenges VR presented, as it removed the interface layer to a great degree. UX for web and mobile applications was mostly centered around the interface and its optimization for user conversion rates.

Classic design and usability engineering principles such as PET—design for persuasion, emotion, and trust—were, all of a sudden, given a completely new meaning in the context of VR. The directness and power of a VR simulation, where all senses are fully exposed to immersive and artificial stimuli, added a new set of responsibilities to the UX designer (Figure 2-3).

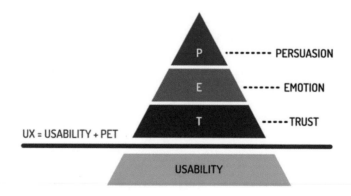

Figure 2-3. *UX is more than usability. Persuasion, emotion, and trust are just as important (image by C. Hillmann)*

With great power comes great responsibility: UX misalignments will have a much greater impact on an immersed user than on a web or mobile app consumer. The visceral nature of VR requires different approaches and wider focus areas in terms of UX. A weak user experience is still considered one of the key barriers to the wider adoption of the technology. UX design for VR goes well beyond addressing usability and designing interaction; it also covers the soft aspects of the experience that can be expressed through PET or persuasion engineering.

UX for VR has made a lot of progress under the leadership of Oculus. The Facebook brand has, since the early days, put a strong emphasis on developing UX guidelines that are based on general best practices, including resting positions, orientation, duration, load times, pace and comfort, as well as more specific areas for visual clues, locomotion, hand interaction, VR sound design, and playtesting. These vast resources are freely available on the Oculus developer website. Frequent updates and blog posts covering progress in critical areas such as research experiments for new locomotion techniques to avoid motion sickness make this an important resource.

2.3.2 Surviving the Hype Curve

The question remains: Why did Oculus fall short of the expectation with its first-generation headsets, the Oculus Rift, the Oculus Go, as well as the Gear VR in partnership with Samsung? Despite having mostly positive media support, an enthusiastic fan base, plus the financial resources of its new owner Facebook, the technology did not take off as expected.

Numerous debates over basic hardware UX concerns, target audiences, and high entry bars for PC VR due to the initial investment required showed that in the end, even the latest generation of VR was not ready for a mass market. In May 2019, more than three years after the Oculus Rift's launch, Oculus released its first 6DOF standalone headset, Oculus Quest, that, with later added option to connect to high-end PC VR, offered the most accessible and most flexible solution to casual users as well as hardcore VR enthusiasts. For many observers, the end of 2019 marks the actual real beginning of the 6DOF VR consumer era.

The modern VR narrative is often centered around Oculus for the reason that Oculus was a first mover in many areas and still is one of the most consistent dedicated brands pushing the technology as part of an expanded social networking strategy within Facebook. Nevertheless, other early pioneers such as HTC Vive, a company that has pivoted toward enterprise applications with HMDs such as the Valve Index, as well as Pimax and HP Reverb based on the Microsoft MR platform, deserve credit for pushing the hardware limits in terms of resolution and FoV, while Sony's Playstation VR made a successful debut in home entertainment, having sold 5 million units by January 2020.

By 2020, the evolution of the VR landscape has been shifting toward inside-out tracking and wireless and standalone headsets. Next up is 5G technology to empower streamed high-end content and the next level of social VR connectivity, as the technology is slowly and steadily gaining user acceptance.

2.3.3 The Apple XR Lineup

Apple has been preparing its market entry for years with tech acquisitions including the recent takeovers of NextVR and Spaces, among others. NextVR has established itself as a technology company for high-quality live and on-demand VR content. The company holds over 40 patents and has successfully streamed music and sports events to a VR headset. Spaces has made its mark as an innovator in the VR video conferencing space. At the time of writing of this book, no wearable Apple XR product has been officially announced, but industry rumors have been indicating that official releases are getting closer to an actual release date. The market entry of Apple will signal a shift toward the XR mass market, and the timing will be carefully chosen by Apple strategists.

Apple's products have always been UX driven, and the Apple wearable XR lineup is expected to set the bar for user comfort, ease of use, and accessibility. Apple market entry into the wearable XR space will be an important market signal to usher in the spatial computing era for consumers on a global scale. For UX designers, this paradigm shift will be an exciting time; it will allow new creative possibilities and room for innovation, taking on the rare opportunities that a major shift in computing platforms brings to design innovators.

2.3.4 VR UX: Usability First

UX design for VR is an ongoing process that is being shaped by the global VR community. VR best practices and standards are not set in stone; instead, they are constantly changing based on input acquired from experiments and updated information using data from failures and success stories. If something works well, the word will spread, and it will find its way into other products.

Usability has been one of the UX priorities for VR since the beginning of the most recent wave of VR innovation. The reason is that VR usability has had to face a lot of issues, such as motion sickness concerns, hardware limitations, and device-related restrictions, in addition to the lack of standards and the great variation of use cases. While maybe still treated as a niche segment when compared to the market shares of consoles and gaming PCs, VR has moved beyond the state of a short-lived trend or fad as predicted by pessimistic analysts. VR has arrived on a long-term growth trajectory and is showing great success in areas such as educational VR and corporate training and enterprise VR, next to having established a loyal gaming fan base. VR is showing consistent growth, reflected by Steam's digital distribution data and increased visibility of enterprise success stories. The growth has also led to an increase in usability knowledge, including a better-equipped toolbox for designers. And, while there has not been one single usability standard, the industries' best practices have been refined to a point where VR usability can be considered a very well-documented focal area, with extensive research, numerous examples, and showcases. The VR market is spearheaded by the usability leaders, which are VR applications that have succeeded through superior usability as an essential part of the UX design and are setting the benchmark for the industry. These examples very often build a frame of reference for successful VR usability.

2.3.5 Setting the Bar for VR Usability

A great reference for excellent VR usability and setting a standard for UX design in VR is the game Half-Life: Alyx, by Valve Corporation, released in March 2020. Based on Half-Life, the celebrated standout IP that revolutionized storytelling in games with its initial release in 1989 and its 2004 groundbreaking sequel, Half-Life 2, the VR-only release of Alyx is designed as a prequel set before the events of Half-Life 2. The title has been praised for its overall game design, interaction concepts, attention to detail, and storytelling. Having earned the critical acclaim as the highest-rated title on the Steam platform, Alyx is regarded by the industry as one of the most ambitious, most complete, and most convincing large-scale immersive entertainment productions that VR has seen up to this point. The title scores with a customizable user experience that builds on the most important UX design features for a satisfying immersive world. For these reasons, the game qualifies as a usability reference and benchmark regarding UX standards.

2.3.6 The Elements of VR Usability

Half-Life: Alyx does usability right. That is an important accomplishment, because a lot of VR titles previously had issues considering the core elements of VR usability. Hardly any of these UX accomplishments are revolutionary; instead, they represent refinement and completeness when it comes to accessibility and interaction options for their features. These elements of usability design are

- – Locomotion

- – Orientation

- – Object interaction

- – Initial setup, onboarding, and accessibility

VR locomotion—options are essential:

Locomotion has had a painful history in VR. Even the contemporary VR era since 2013 has been troubled by a user segment that suffers from motion sickness, also referred to as simulation sickness. Data from decades of simulation research shows that about 25–40 percent of first-time VR users have an initial simulation sickness reaction that goes away over time, while a very small 3–5 percentage has a simulation sickness reaction that is persistent. This data, plus media reports of a general simulation sickness problem of VR, had initially made developers decide to use teleportation as the preferred locomotion method in VR. That decision was rejected by a lot of VR gamers, who felt that teleportation didn't work for their gameplay style. In turn, they demanded classic thumbstick control, often called smooth locomotion, to be used in the same way as in traditional first-person shooters and other action games. The solution to this dilemma has been surprisingly simple: offering both as an option and letting the user decide (through the game options) what style of locomotion is preferred—teleportation-style movement for users with motion sickness problems and FPS-style smooth locomotion for gamers without motion sickness issues. Offering this option has now been established as a usability standard and best practice in VR for cases where the gameplay is not tied to a specific locomotion style. Providing locomotion options to the user and letting the individual choose a preferred style, according to personal preference, opens the door to as many users as possible, no matter the player type. The choices of locomotion are

Teleportation with screen fade:

A fade-out at start and a fade-in by reaching the teleportation destination makes this the most comfortable setting for sensitive users; it is the default in Alyx and called Blink in the game. With Blink you can set the destination orientation before teleporting. Small movement adjustments with the analog stick can be customized in the preference options.

Fast linear movement:

Zapping with a fast linear movement from the current position to a selected destination is known to eliminate motion sickness. The reason is that simulation sickness based on the sensory mismatch theory (visual stimuli in conflict with vestibular feedback) is eliminated when high speed is used, transitioning through a space.

Smooth locomotion:

Smooth locomotion is the closest to conventional first-person games and most often the preferred locomotion type for experienced VR gamers. It offers the most immersive experience due to the fact that the exploration of space is experienced as a spatial perception through visual movement parallax. Alyx offers smooth locomotion options based on head orientation and on hand orientation. The title refers to smooth locomotion as *continuous movement.*

Locomotion options for different user types, from beginners or the motion sickness sensitive to experienced gamers with "VR legs," are an essential ingredient for an inclusive UX design.

Orientation—snap rotation is important:

Throughout the recent design history of best practices for a VR experience, orientation settings and controls had often enjoyed a lesser priority. Developers often assumed that the user would be standing up during the experience and that body rotation should be done in the natural way, insisting that natural body rotation would offer a more immersive simulation. Based on these assumptions, artificial rotation by analog stick was labeled immersion breaking. It turned out that this assumption was wrong. VR users don't experience snap rotation, which is the most common rotation type, as immersion breaking; instead, they consider it an essential tool to reorient during gameplay. In addition to that, there are situations where users are unable to turn, because they are seated, for example, in an airplane, or are restricted in their motion by location constraints or by disabilities. A large percentage of users prefer a seated VR experience, especially when it comes to longer sessions or VR media consumption. Snap rotation has been proven to work for these situations. The fast rotational movement that snaps to fixed angles has also been proven to be free of motion sickness concerns.

The takeaway for VR usability is that snap rotation should be available, even if it is initially disabled and needs to be activated in the user's game options. Snap rotation is such an essential ingredient that, if not available, it can ruin an otherwise positive VR experience. A lot of VR titles allow snap rotation to be customized, between different snapping angles and style options, such as smooth rotation vs. angle snap. At its very basic level, snap rotation with a 15° angle will help the user to reorient when necessary, without making a VR title unplayable in certain situations. It is an option that is very easy to implement, and every VR title should have it. Alyx goes as far as offering snap angles from 15 to 90 degrees in 15-degree increments and in addition offers the option for smooth rotation with a variable speed setting.

Object interaction—making it fun and intuitive:

Valve's Alyx is a great reference for intuitive VR object interaction. For a VR game that requires a lot of object exploration and inspection, often in hard-to-reach places, it is important to be able to "force pull" objects from the distance into the user's hands for inspection, in order to keep the pacing of the action flowing. This "gravity pull" solution has been established in a number of VR titles to overcome the otherwise time-consuming and cumbersome task to move to every item and pick it up as one would in real life. Adding the VR force pull ability, in Alyx called "gravity glove," makes the game flow intuitive, fun, and uninterrupted. In addition to the basic force pull feature, the gravity gloves also require a bit of low-level skill. To be able to catch the item, the user has to flip the wrist and then catch it with the right timing. It requires some practice, but at the same time adds a bit of gameplay to a repetitive task, turning it into a satisfying and enjoyable game mechanic.

Object inventory gestures are designed in a very intuitive and accessible way in Alyx. To store picked-up ammunition, the user throws it behind into an imaginary backpack, with a hand gesture. To reach into the inventory, the user grabs behind themselves, bringing the item forward.

Object interaction is the bread and butter of a VR experience. To be able to grab an object, interact with it, store it, retrieve it, and change its attributes are the essential parts where usability plays a crucial role. Alyx shows how it is done right in a sci-fi game environment, but at the same time sets a usability reference that might as well be used in any VR project, may it be educational or enterprise VR.

Initial setup and accessibility:

Initial setup helps to cater to different user types and their preferences. To be able to choose between standing and seated gameplay types means setting height adjust and crouch action settings, to compensate for the lost height in a seated position vs. a standing position only. Additional options for one-handed gameplay, right- vs. left-handed modes, difficulty levels, as well as settings for players with disabilities make it an inclusive and accessible title that makes it appeal to all types of players.

2.3.7 Alyx: The Gold Standard for VR Usability

The evolution of VR standards has shown that best practices are constantly evolving based on user feedback and ultimately on the success of the product and its rating. Alyx is a critically acclaimed premium product, and one of the world's most cherished IPs, built by a company that was instrumental in lifting the latest wave of VR technology off the ground.

This gives enough reason to consider Alyx a future reference framework, in terms of usability, options, and customization, for VR-based experiences. Giving the user options for the key ingredient of setup, locomotion, and orientation is essential, unless a VR project is tied to limiting mechanics that make these options redundant, impossible, or unnecessary. Surprisingly few VR titles offer the basic set of options that Alyx allows. A large percentage of VR titles still don't offer snap rotation, and only a few give smooth locomotion as an option other than teleportation.

Best practices and usability standards in VR will without question evolve further over time. UX research processes such as user testing can help to bring more insights into an area that doesn't have a fixed set of rules and often is still experimental in nature. Nevertheless, reference titles such as Alyx help to guide the way by setting usability standards that can be expanded in the future.

2.3.8 Designing the VR Future, Beyond Usability

Usability is only one part of UX design, but in VR it plays a crucial role. It has to be right before the other UX design building blocks can fall into place. The UX considerations that make an experience valuable, meaningful, and emotionally satisfying have to be built on a solid usability framework.

The good news is that better tools, improved technology, and more unified standards will help designers in the near future, as the technology progresses. Some of the important trends that will impact UX design for VR are

Unified standards:

The official introduction of OpenXR 1.0 in 2019 can be considered a first important step in making development and porting between platforms easier for designers and developers. OpenXR solves the fragmentation problem of XR platforms, engines, and technologies. OpenXR application and device interface layers allow apps from any engine or platform to target any VR headset. This standardization will also help streamline best practices and standards concerning controller mapping and interaction design in general. We should expect unified standards, for example, regarding button mappings, leading to unified frameworks for UX and prototyping, making cross-platform play and testing easier, faster, and better to communicate.

Improved technology for a higher-quality experience:

A lighter headset with more comfort, a higher resolution, and a wider field of view are expected to roll out over the next years. Better quality and comfort mean longer sessions are not a problem, and current problems with the readability of small text will help the long-term vision of an XR-based virtual office. We can expect eye tracking and varifocal optics to enhance visual quality and open new opportunities for social VR, with eye communication.

VR as part of a wireless and social XR future:

The preferred VR experience in the decade ahead and beyond will be wireless. The arrival of 5G networks is expected to use cloud-enabled social VR, not only for entertainment but for the virtual office as well. Virtual co-working and avatar-based meetings are expected to revolutionize the workplace. WebVR, next to WebAR (also referred to as WebXR), is expected to continue growing as a widely available platform without barriers and gatekeepers. We can expect more immersive virtual replica and VR room reconstruction and persistent shareable virtual objects. More and more things will have a digital twin with a VR access point.

From XR convergence to the brain-computer interface (BCI):

VR and AR are expected to converge into a flexible XR wearable device. The forerunners of this convergence have already been tested in both device categories. AR functions in VR headsets have been established with VR passthrough options, while in turn VR on AR devices has been successfully enabled by turning the transparent glasses opaque. To merge these experimental functions into an XR device that can do both, AR and VR, is the next logical and evolutionary step. A single spatial experience in XR has the potential to be shared between different wearable AR and VR device types and all-in-one XR HMDs, as well as giving access points to handheld mobile spectator screens. In addition to that, we can expect better and extended haptics and more options to include human senses, in the near future. Current, noninvasive brain-computer interface (BCI) research shows promise in enhancing world interaction and navigation with the additional help of machine learning. The most likely introduction of BCI will be to assist with hand and controller interaction, enabling neuro-assisted, hands-free communication, reducing barriers for the disabled in addition to making interactions faster and more intuitive.

2.3.9 User-Centric Design in a Changing Digital Environment

It is no question that XR is part of the disruption by Industry 4.0 and its wider implications in the consumer market. The revolution in the manufacturing process mirrors the digital transformation at the workplace and at home, where XR will increasingly tie into everyday activities, such as communication, education, and ecommerce.

The role of UX design in this process is to keep the focus on the user's needs, advocate accessibility and usability standards, and take user agency through the constantly changing digital landscape, putting the user at the center of this transformation and creating solutions that turn these needs into meaningful experiences.

To be able to address these areas, UX designers need a deeper understanding of what is possible in XR and what tools are available to fix problems, if they occur in the design process for a digital XR product.

The good news is that due to the dynamic environment of the industry, we are seeing new tools that make these tasks easier. One example is the application Microsoft Maquette that helps with the ideation and prototyping process for XR. Maquette lets the XR designer sketch out ideas for AR and VR and create mockups and thus allows them to communicate concepts to stakeholders and clients. We will most likely see more of these types of prototyping tools in the near future, reflecting a growing XR design ecosystem.

2.3.10 VR Usability Heuristics

After looking at the bigger picture of how VR evolves within the emerging XR industry, what role usability elements play in the context of interaction design, it is important to evaluate what methods can be used to analyze usability feedback in a structured manner according to heuristic evaluations.

Heuristics means, using a rule of thumb or an educated guess, as a shortcut for a solution. One of the best methods is to use the ten usability heuristics for user interface design by Jakob Nielsen.

Using these as a blueprint to evaluate VR interface design and usability is a good starting point. They are in short form

> 1: Visibility of system status (keep the user informed)

> 2: Match between the system and the real world (speak the user's language)

> 3: User control and freedom (help the user avoid unwanted situations)

> 4: Consistency and standards (follow conventions)

> 5: Error prevention (present users with confirmation options)

> 6: Recognition rather than recall (minimize the user's memory load)

> 7: Flexibility and efficiency of use (cater to beginners and advanced users)

> 8: Aesthetic and minimalist design (eliminate irrelevant information)

> 9: Help users recognize, diagnose, and recover from errors (communicate problems and solutions clearly)

> 10: Help and documentation (make it easy to search for answers)

The benefit of this approach is to keep an eye on best practices for usability and interface design while evaluating how VR solutions hold up to general UX standards in comparison. Next to general user interface heuristics by Jakob Nielsen, there are a number of VR usability heuristics that are often highly subjective, platform dependent, and sometimes based on quickly outdated assumptions, due to the constantly changing XR landscape. Nevertheless, it makes sense to check the latest research and consider heuristics based on the targeted device and use case.

2.3.11 UX: Storyboarding, Ideation, and User Journey Maps for VR

The UX design process for XR products is still highly experimental. While the method and its principles are unchanged, it is the practical implementation that is still in a process of refinement. Some obvious questions typically arise: If a design sprint requires a mid-fidelity prototype, what is the best solution? Some areas of the UX design process that have been established with web and mobile app design can easily be transferred to the XR design process, whereas other processes, such as prototyping, are not as easily transferable to spatial design. Instead of using traditional wireframing, the space allocation of content modules, and its prioritization and behavior for 2D screens, it makes more sense to use a 3D storyboard approach to capture the 3D, spatial storytelling aspect of a VR experience. For the UX ideation process, it makes sense to use a 3D design tool such as Blender or one of the UX and design applications that are already available in VR, such as Gravity Sketch or Microsoft Marquette. User journey maps and the UX process in which they are used can be transferred to VR, but with different priorities.

2.3.12 Future-Proofing Design Methods

Taking the bigger XR picture into account allows the XR designer to focus on the core benefits of designing for spatial computing beyond the current headset generations or favorite feature flavor. While usability heuristics and best practices are good solutions in the short run, they may be outlived soon. For that reason, it is important to have a strong emphasis on method and system thinking. Having a resilient purpose while practicing efficiency helps in focusing on the basic design principles that are inherent to all digital media, including XR applications. UX design methods are universal and apply to the design of a kitchen table as much as to the design of a VR flight simulator. The methods, principles, and processes of UX design are inherently the same for any type of product. Nevertheless, on the practical level, the industry, sector, and device heuristics, together with the best practices, are constantly changing. For example, VR heuristics can occasionally be too narrow or too general, and important aspects that hardly ever impose a problem in the wider digital media design field require much more attention in VR. One example is the role of typography and text readability, which has plagued VR from the very beginning due to technical limitations. To prevent overlooking these kinds of problems, it is often a good idea to take a step back and consider Nielson's usability goals: learnability, efficiency, memorability, error prevention, and satisfaction. Applying these goals as guiding principles in the usability evaluation process is a sure way to keep track of the long-term goals of designing a successful XR experience.

2.4 AR: Handheld AR Success Stories, Prototypes, and the AR Cloud

Handheld AR using mobile phones or tablets has already entered mainstream through filter overlays by messaging apps such as Snapchat and casual games such as the often quoted Pokemon Go. The technology has also found its way into rear-parking assistants for cars, guiding the driver with the vehicle's projected trajectory around obstacles, through the rear camera's video monitor with an AR overlay.

These examples demonstrate that the entry level, to provide a useful interaction application for the user, starts with fairly low technical minimum requirements. The technical requirements for AR glasses, such as the Microsoft HoloLens (Figure 2-4), that allow the user to interact with a stereoscopic hologram within the environment are much more sophisticated in nature.

Figure 2-4. *The Microsoft HoloLens 2 (image by C. Hillmann)*

The required information for a high-end AR application to fully understand the user's environment entails a number of complex tasks. The AR app has to fully understand and interpret each individual user's unique environment situation, if an aesthetically pleasing and meaningful interaction of AR components with environment objects is required. Computer vision is used for 3D reconstruction and semantic segmentation to understand the scene's context for modification. The process of

51

detecting, registering, tracking, and interpreting a space, its depth information and resulting occlusion, plus the nature of objects, surfaces, their material properties, and the lightning condition they are in, is an intricate computational endeavor. AR sensor technology has a lot to cover, considering that an application has to work in any unique space, from an industrial warehouse to a cluttered kitchen.

The variety of environment situations is fundamental to UX design: While for VR development, the environment layout is entirely up to the designer to create, in AR it is dependent on the individual situation of the user's actual surroundings.

On a long shot, we expect AR to be able to understand and identify any individual object and any possible environment situation through machine learning. This is of course a major challenge, due to the endless object and surface variety and the overall complexity of the natural environment, including organic items that move, deform, and constantly change.

In its current state, AR works best when it is focused on a limited subset of environment features. At this point, they are flat and angled surface areas considering depth and occlusion, in addition to predefined patterns through markers or objects.

2.4.1 AR Application Types and Device Categories

Even though AR devices can be dramatically different, considering handheld phones and tablets and wearable AR glasses like the Microsoft HoloLens, the main AR application types are consistent across all device categories. These types are

a) Marker-based AR:

Markers are unique patterns that an AR app can recognize and use as a trigger. Markers can be QR codes or distinct predefined design patterns that the app uses as an anchor. Examples are AR enhanced books with extended 3D content enabled by markers on book pages.

b) Markerless AR:

Markerless uses the SLAM (simultaneous localization and mapping) process, for placing content in the environment. One example is the *IKEA Place* app that lets users try furniture designs in their own home environment using markerless AR.

c) Location-based AR:

Digital AR content that requires a GPS, compass, accelerometer, or any other position system that falls under location-based AR. Virtual objects are tied to a specific location, for example, guided maps, cultural and heritage guides, as well as AR location-based games, such as the famous Pokemon Go title.

These three AR application types can be used with either device category, if the application is designed for it:

1. A handheld mobile AR device such as a tablet or mobile phone

2. An AR headset, such as the Magic Leap 1 or the Microsoft HoloLens

The most important distinction for UX designers, next to AR type, is by device category: handheld AR or wearable AR glasses. Interaction design on handheld AR devices follows, to a great degree, the established UX/UI design set of rules for mobile and web applications, while wearable AR glasses, enabling stereoscopic perception and gesture or controller interaction, follow the spatial interaction ruleset that is closer to the UX conventions of VR.

The targeted design solutions for interactive content are fundamentally different for each case: on a handheld AR device, by touch controls using the screen, or on an AR headset with gestures or handheld controllers, by interacting within the projected 3D space.

2.4.2 Projection-Based AR

There is one AR category that lives outside of these device categories, application types, and use cases: It is called projection-based AR or projected AR. Projection-based AR systems allow the user to interact with a projected image through gestures or by other input methods. The use cases range from windshield AR for cars, as an intelligent driver's assistance, to large-scale art installations where it is often used in conjunction with projection mapping. Projected AR has a long history and used to be the most common and most visible form of AR. A number of projected AR use cases will be replaced once AR glasses become more commonly used, for the reason that any projection can theoretically be simulated within an AR HMD.

The rest of projected AR applications remain a highly specialized niche, very often focused on experimental live performances or unique events, where a custom installation interacts with visitors in a confined space.

UX designers specializing in projected AR often work with the software TouchDesigner and specialized motion capture devices such as the Microsoft Kinect to create immersive and interactive real-time content. The software uses a node-based visual scripting language and is very flexible in supporting numerous audio-visual input methods to drive its media system.

This AR type is not intended to run on standardized hardware for a mass audience and, therefore, will not be covered in this book. It is a highly specialized area that requires its own dedicated documentation for its unique requirements, problems, and use cases. Nevertheless, it is a rewarding area for UX designers who are willing to specialize in that field.

2.4.3 The AR Road Map

One challenge for UX designers in the AR field is the variety of devices with different capabilities. Some AR devices are equipped with better sensors than others. One example is the LiDAR (Light Detection and Ranging) scanner on Apple's recent line of iPads and iPhones. The LiDAR scanner brings more precision to capturing a room's 3D characteristics and thus enables much better occlusion on objects that are embedded in the environment. The result is a much more convincing and realistic perception of objects that are covered by real-life objects, in essence much better precision with occlusion on the intersection of the real environment and the virtual AR object. In applications or games where occlusion plays an important role, this enhancement can be a make or break feature. Enhancing standard mobile device features with specialized hardware was first done by Google with Project Tango in 2014. Even though phones integrating the special 3D sensors delivered superior results, Project Tango was shut down in 2017, and Google shifted its focus to the software-only platform ARCore, the competitor of Apple's ARKit, due to the fact that it would scale much better and reach potentially every mobile device.

Basically, all modern phones and tablets are AR capable to some degree, but there is no specified standard that classifies a handheld as "AR ready" to set a minimum bar for technical specs required to guarantee a quality experience.

Another challenge for UX designers is the fact that the AR world is in the early stages of a transition from handheld AR to wearable AR using headsets. While the majority of AR apps are designed for handheld only, it is probably a good idea to keep an eye on a design solution that makes the transition from a handheld screen interaction to a spatial interaction with an AR headset based on the same AR content smooth and consistent. The decade ahead is expected to streamline the wide variation of devices and technologies, and the UX designer's role is to advocate the user-centric perspective, to guarantee accessibility and inclusion of as many user types as possible.

2.4.4 AR Success Stories

Handheld AR applications have had a number of well-documented success stories since 2013, when its modern use was introduced. Marker-based AR found its way into print products, in its earliest form with a QR code, to enhance the content by triggering multimedia clips in the context of the printed image. An additional 3D view of a 2D image adds value, especially in educational context. Comic books have used marker-based AR successfully to add animation sequences to the static page images. Children's books with added AR content have been very popular and successful, because they allow children to dive deeper into a story and thus increase the learning potential. AR has often been used as a training extension for technically complex hardware as well as consumer product explainers. Mercedes-Benz introduced AR-based manuals in 2018. The AR manual app called "Ask Mercedes" explains the car's features with a contextual and interactive AR layer on a mobile phone or tablet. Educational AR has been proven to work, often providing a contextual learning assistance for static documentation, for example, with training on industrial machinery, where the marker-based AR approach offers an easy solution for quick access to the operational context.

One of the social media pioneers of markerless AR is the app Snapchat. Enabling AR-embedded 3D objects for camera-captured environments and tracked portrait video overlays became one of the most popular use cases for AR in a social media context. A success story that inspired other messaging services including Facebook and Instagram.

Location-based AR was most widely popularized by Google Maps, which allowed to follow environment-embedded way markers to guide the user to a destination. Typical examples for contemporary AR-enabled ecommerce are apps that let consumers try out cosmetics, tattoos, hats, or accessories using a smartphone camera. Remote assistance to help with technical problems in the enterprise field has been pioneered with Vuforia Chalk, as an easy-to-implement AR solution. One of the most visible showcases for AR is still the previously mentioned *IKEA Place* app that lets users try out virtual furniture in their home environment. Handheld AR has shown to solve real-world problems. The upcoming generation of consumer-grade AR HMDs will most likely accelerate this development and show these benefits in a more immersed stereoscopic view.

2.4.5 UX Design for AR Spaces

UX design for handheld AR has to consider the fact that the environment is part of the design context. This fact makes it different from mobile and web design approaches, where the interaction is limited to a screen and the app's UI. Another important aspect is that AR objects live in a 3D world. This means objects have to be designed as 3D geometry. Even if the object is a 2D plane, it is still placed within a 3D context and can often be viewed from different 3D viewing angles; as a consequence, its 3D context has to be considered.

Specific solutions like environment guidance for users and off-screen object notification are often required to make sure the flow is not interrupted. The 3D content and the possible trigger animations need to be designed in a way that works in AR. To help with prototyping, an increasing variety of AR design apps have helped streamline the process that would otherwise be very technical if only using Unity or Unreal with ARCore and ARKit as a starting point.

Adobe Aero, for example, enables UX design prototyping and testing for user interaction within an environment using imported 3D objects. The application allows the testing and fine-tuning of typical object properties, such as trigger types and trigger actions. This allows UX designers to evaluate 3D design choices that can then be adjusted according to the test results. More complex web-based production and prototyping tools such as the Sumerian application by AWS provide an even more complete prototyping solution using visual scripting for interaction design, while the prototyping app Microsoft Marquette is a sophisticated tool for spatial ideation in XR.

At a basic level, AR prototyping tools provide a sandbox for planning out the core components, spatial layout, UI, and object components to test an idea or concept. Being able to sketch out ideas for onboarding, user flow, and UI interaction using these tools is a helpful shortcut in the development process. Ideation and prototyping play an important role in AR, as small changes in the 3D environment can have a dramatic impact. Fine-tuning and testing is required when the position or size of a placed AR object is important. Visual stimuli, such as animations, help to signal if an object has changed its properties, has become active, or is awaiting action. Voice and sound in general may help with navigation and assistance. User testing helps to evaluate if the AR design is delivering the expected outcome. Compared to UX/UI web and mobile design best practices, users may find it hard to rotate objects, readjust the view, or navigate active items. Therefore, a visual language that is able to assist with the application's usability has to be part of the design solution. The additional responsibilities and possible pitfalls are manifold, when comparing UX design for digital AR products with UX approaches for mobile and web applications.

Wearable AR is without question an emerging industry, but while technology and use cases give a good picture on how the wider adoption will develop over time, it remains unclear how and to what degree consumers will embrace it. User preference and market sentiment can, at times, be hard to predict. To illustrate that point, one can look at the failure of the first Google Glass consumer release in 2013. The device, a cutting-edge AR wearable at the time, with a number of advanced and useful features, among them location-aware notifications, was rejected entirely by the wider market. The failure of Google Glass was an important lesson for UX designers that unexpected things can happen or lower-priority items can become a big issue. In this case, the sociocultural aspect of the user experience was brought to the forefront. An AR device needs to be socially acceptable to be used comfortably. Any device has to be tested for its social interaction, which is a major responsibility for UX design. Google Glass did not succeed in that area; the negative perception of Google Glass was driven by concerns of privacy intrusion through the outfacing camera. The backlash was a major setback for the project, and it started a heated debate over its possible UX flaws and unclear user benefits, besides the controversy over its camera. The step from handheld AR to wearable AR headsets is a huge transition for UX designers, and the examples of the issues surrounding the original Google Glass show that UX problems can occur in areas where no one expected them. Using a wearable AR device may have unwanted side effects that could become a problem when used in a public space. Certain actions or gestures may not be socially acceptable, or not inclusive, or could be considered unsafe in public, for example, in traffic, or any place where accidents can occur. There are a number of examples that show how important it is to take a holistic view of UX design for AR beyond product design, and Google Glass is a prime example of that.

Very often it helps to look beyond the technology and think about what a human experience is all about and what factors contribute to that experience in a positive way. A comparison to an emerging technology is the idea of entering an unknown country. What information and assistance do I need to feel comfortable and safe, how do I get around, and what should I watch out for to not offend anyone and blend in? What information is available up front so that I can enter with confidence? UX researchers have used role play to act out what happens in a user experience. To observe motivations and habits in role play is a good way to explore the subject in a technology-agnostic way. UX researchers take this opportunity to deep dive into the humanities to explore the deeper ties to behavioral patterns and how they relate to a holistic view of an experience.

2.4.5.1 Privacy UX

Privacy is part of UX or, let's better say, has become part of UX. While privacy used to be an afterthought a decade ago, it has now moved to the front row, due to the changing social media landscape. Users want to be able to control where and when their data is being used and by whom and what options they may have to restrict access to their personal information. Privacy UX is now playing a major role in how a user feels about a digital product.

Google Glass was the first product that had triggered a lot of questions on privacy and AR. As a result, Google has pivoted the product away from the consumer to the enterprise market. The Google Glass enterprise edition is now focusing on the manufacturing workplace with a head-up display to provide contextual information with computer vision and machine learning.

The Google Glass privacy disaster shows that AR technology touches a lot of sensitive areas concerning data privacy. It shows how important it is for headset developers to communicate their privacy concept.

The fact that AR technology is based on the concept of constantly scanning and analyzing an environment and sending that information online is a potential privacy nightmare. Consumers have legitimate concerns about how, where, in what form, and how long that data is stored. If a user's private apartment is scanned by an AR device, including details that they may not wish to share, how is it guaranteed that this information, in case it is required for the system to run, is kept safe, encrypted, and private on a remote server? Microsoft has stated that it addressed this problem by obfuscating the collected data, so 3D point clouds and localization information are concealed and, without loss of performance or accuracy, cannot be abused.

Facebook Reality Labs is acknowledging the widely shared concerns about data privacy, in the Project Aria guidelines. Project Aria, the research project to collect data to be used in the upcoming Facebook AR cloud called Live Maps, was created to develop the safeguards and policies next to the technical infrastructure, as a step toward the AR cloud to be interfacing with the upcoming Facebook AR glasses. Project Aria's data collection runs through a privacy filter that automatically blurs faces and license plates.

The big idea behind the AR cloud is an interconnected digital twin of everything, in a way the equivalent of Google Maps, but in a much larger, more detailed way, enabling personalized and contextualized assistance. The AR cloud is often called mirror world, but also goes by various other names. Magic Leap named it the Magicverse; Facebook labeled it Live Maps. It is the data infrastructure of the spatial computing future, allowing an augmented layer over reality. In a way it means moving the Internet from screens into the actual environment. The AR cloud is a large-scale infrastructure project that will take years to become a natural part of everyday life. While this development has been the subject of dystopian fears, considering an environment with an autonomous AI, Internet of Things, and blockchain infrastructure, it is in the same way an opportunity for education, learning, market access for small businesses, and making remote work more productive. At the same time, the AR cloud vision touches a lot of questions that are relevant to UX design—data sharing and privacy being in the front row of the most pressing concerns from the user's perspective.

The most obvious benefit of the AR cloud is the concept of shared data in a spatial digital environment. Digital objects can be shared in public or among groups of users, in the same way that people put Post-it notes on real-world items. Persistent digital objects in AR can communicate ideas with visual clues, but in addition to that, allow functions to enable transactions and revolutionize the way a user perceives and interacts with the world around them. Persistent digital objects are enabled through Google's ARCore Cloud Anchors and Apple's ARKit Location Anchors, as well as the more loosely defined persistence in geolocation tags that only gives a rough geospatial augmentation without the precise depth map positioning. The use cases for persistent digital objects can be anything from virtual and shared monitors at the workplace to extended content that spreads around screens of home entertainment systems. Once comfort, visual quality, and field of view get to a point that AR wearables become a part of daily life, the next level will be the AR remapping, or sometimes called reskinning, of the user's environment. Placing a virtual painting on an otherwise empty wall could potentially be almost as good as the real thing if the technology is convincing enough. AR remapping could go as far as switching the appearance of interiors including furniture, opening the door to an AR reskinning economy, offering AR furniture and interior skins to enhance the AR environment—replacing a set of drawers with an antique cabinet of the same dimensions but as a digital overlay, for example, if the technology supports a convincing selective opacity system. The user would enjoy the same haptics interacting with a real physical object but with a different appearance in AR. VR enthusiasts have done similar experiments with room-scale VR, reconstructing their apartments in 3D and mapping it to the precise dimensions of the real world. Replacing the furniture with digital counterparts has the advantage of the same haptic realism that is often used in VR arcades. The potential of remapping is nothing less than spectacular and one of the big promises of an XR future.

Persistent AR objects that are shared in the AR cloud can be considered the foundation for the new XR economy of digital and spatial goods. We can expect multiple AR clouds to compete for the consumer in the same way as the digital economy today is divided through competing platforms.

One aspect of the AR evolution is also its interaction with VR applications using the same digital infrastructure and spatial data. In the long run, the transition from AR to VR and vice versa is expected to be fluid. Merging the features and capabilities of AR and VR into one do-it-all XR device seems like a logical step at some point in the future, once the technical hurdles concerning comfort, resolution, and FoV are resolved. Tuning in and out of VR when needed while being in AR most of the time would certainly make sense. The challenges for UX design in this environment are to measure and apply what is best for the user, considering the key attributes that are driving this experience and keeping pace with the evolution of the user's priorities. In the end it is about making complicated things easier and understanding the user's paint points, behaviors, goals, and needs over time—goals, needs and priorities that can change over time, as the growing concern for data security has shown.

2.5 A New Era of XR Gamification: UX and User Engagement

The rise of UX design and the emerging XR ecosystem has been complemented by the success of gamification, a mega trend in motivational information systems. Gamification is the use of game mechanics and game design principles in a non-game context to improve user engagement. There are a number of reasons why gamification plays an important role for XR applications to attract and retain users. First of all, gamification works. It is an undisputed success story since the wider concept became popular in 2002, when game designer Nick Pelling created the term to apply game mechanics such as points, rewards, and batches, among others, to non-gaming applications. Parallel to that, also around 2002, a new branch of the game industry, called serious games, established itself as a solution for educational simulation and behavior training. Serious games are games that have been designed for training or learning purposes instead of entertainment, very often used for crisis simulation, forensic investigations, and evacuation training, for example. While the serious game industry is still a niche, gamification has taken the world by storm and since 2010 made its way into fitness, education, and almost every area where motivation and engagement is critical. Gamification has changed the world and is even making its way into civic engagement and GovTech. A trend that is occasionally not without controversy, as the Chinese "social credit" system that uses gamification on its citizens to earn trust points. Nevertheless, gamification and techniques such as using gamified avatars in elearning and social media engagement have been a tremendous success.

Gamification has become mainstream, and it has become a tool for XR designers to create user engagement by building systems that motivate and assist users through an experience (Figure 2-5).

Figure 2-5. *The gamification pipeline (C. Hillmann)*

Gamification has also matured to a point where it is not just the stereotypical mechanics using leaderboards and achievements, but also more subtle forms that serve a similar goal, but with less obvious elements.

One of the reasons for that is gamification elements have to work in the context of subjects where fun elements would be out of place. For example, the gamification of a UX design that would cover a medical procedure would have to reflect the situation of the user. Subtle gamification uses the core elements of gamification, establishing a goal and a ruleset as part of the UX design and thus motivating behaviors to successfully master and complete the experience.

Instead of a bouncy coin, as an example for a typical gamification icon in an ecommerce application, the visual language would have to be adjusted to the mood and character of the digital product. Subtle checkmarks for completed areas and visual signals that a section of the product has been successfully explored can reaffirm the user with gamification mechanics that are not very obvious but nevertheless effective in assisting the user.

In the case of XR, a technology that is still relatively new to a lot of people, gamification can help in orientation, affirmation, and onboarding for XR products. New XR users typically worry that they are facing the wrong way or look at the wrong thing, or they are often unsure if the performed action was right. Digital objects in a spatial XR environment are often scattered in 360 degrees and can lead to discovery problems or usability flaws when the user is unsure about orientation and goals of an application.

Gamification can be an important tool for UX designers to address the issues that come with the spatial design nature of an XR experience. But it should also be noted that gamification adds a whole new layer of complexity to a design and can be a budget question in many cases. Game mechanics have to be designed, implemented, and tested, in addition to the UX basics.

2.5.1 The XR Gamification Layer

To add the subtle intrinsic excitement of gamification as a UX design layer for an XR project, we need to look at the key ingredients of gamification, which are

- Motivation

- Mastery

- Triggers

Motivation:

Motivation is the force that drives the user's behavior to earn rewards, such as satisfaction, happiness, and positive feelings, but also badges, trophies, and rankings. The key question here is "Why are we doing things?"

Mastery:

Mastery is the process of acquiring a skill and with it the feeling of accomplishment. As we progress through the game mechanics, adding knowledge through persistence, we get a sense of mastery and the sensation of overcoming a challenge to complete a task. The key question is here: "How are we doing things?"

Triggers:

Triggers are signals to prompt the user to *act now*. A trigger is implemented to instruct the user to complete a target behavior at the right time, in order to direct a user's behavioral response. The trigger creates a positive feedback at a specific critical point in time, for example, when the user may be less engaged. The key question for triggers is: "When are we doing things?"

2.5.2 The XR Gamification Toolset

An established gamification framework is usually the best first step to approach the gamification of an XR product. A framework, like the popular Octalysis system, allows to analyze the driving forces of human motivation in relation to the product's goals, on a high-concept level. By identifying the core behavioral drivers, it is then possible to conceptualize and prototype the actual game mechanics. Fortunately, XR development tools are based on game engines with gamification components as part of the core technology and therefore very accessible. Both the Unreal and the Unity game engine feature easy-to-implement gameplay functions that can be used, not only for games but for gamification as well. A typical example is the progress bar, a core component in games, very often used as a health bar or to show ammunition amount and general power charge. The progress bar is one of the gamification elements that has made its way into a lot of everyday processes. Online registrations for web-based services are typically accompanied by a progress bar to show how much of the personal profile information is complete and what elements are missing. The progress bar is a powerful visual signal that motivates the user to finish the task, by showing how close in percentage the final goal actually is. The psychology behind this process is the feeling of accomplishment once the task is completed. When a task is completed, the brain releases endorphins as a reward, which in turn create the feeling of happiness and satisfaction. Once we complete the required task and reach the goal, we feel good about achieving something. The human mind has a deep-seated urge to clean things up, get it done, and tidy up, and the progress bar gives us a visual incentive to do so. If we don't follow that urge, we may be left with a feeling of incompleteness, which causes tension or stress, even if it is only on a very subtle level.

The progress bar can of course have many different forms, like a task list or power meter, as well as level indicator. It has both a negative stimulus and a positive reinforcement: the negative being an uncompleted status and the positive the accomplishment. Once the full accomplishment has been reached, it may trigger another gamification component, the badge or trophy, in its numerous variations.

2.5.3 XR Onboarding with Gamification

The progress bar is a good example for a useful core component when it comes to onboarding in XR. As an emerging technology, XR applications are still new to a large percentage of the population. Compared to established mobile technologies where users are familiar with the interaction standards, such as touch gestures, the inexperienced XR user could feel unsure and uneasy about the onboarding process for an XR application. Gamification plays an important role here, as it helps to direct the user's attention with reassurance and motivation. Other typical examples are introduction tutorial levels for VR applications that teach the basics, such as locomotion and object interactions with a gamified guide. The typical gamification tools of using progress bars, badges, and trophies, once tutorial sections have been completed, have been proven to work well in an XR context. One of the best examples is the Oculus onboarding app *First Steps* that introduces new users to VR in an entertaining, playful, and engaging way while introducing the device's features and conventions.

2.5.4 VR and Gamification

Simulation-based training has had very good success with using a combination of VR and gamification. To learn new skills and behaviors, VR offers a new opportunity and novel approach to give a realistic feel to a learning situation. Educational VR applications with game mechanics often enable a scaffolding approach to the learning material while taking advantage of the immersive and secluded nature of the VR experience. This approach has been successfully used in medical learning using gamification to spot correct answers during training. Medical learning is a good example where playful interaction is very effective in VR, as the focus object can be brought up close and enlarged to identify the area of interest while still having an eye on the object's context. Immersive VR learning using scores, badges, trophies, and rankings has been proven to enhance the learning experience, increase user engagement, and improve the learning result. VR learning is a success story that is expected to expand further into other areas where a simulated environment is important, such as corporate and safety training.

Another area where XR gamification plays a major role is VR fitness. Fitness has been a natural use case for VR due to the spatial nature of the technology. Moving the body with a VR HMD has a lot of potential to optimize a training, due to its motion tracking data and resulting feedback. VR for fitness is an obvious future market and an opportunity for developers. The factors that work against it, headset discomfort, sweat removal, and hygiene, will get better over time, once headsets become more lightweight and easier to clean. In the meantime, disposable VR covers that absorb sweat have become an acceptable solution for VR fitness enthusiasts. An enthusiastic and dedicated VR fitness community spearheaded by focused news sites such as vrfitnessinsider.com helps to keep track of the latest developments and innovate fitness gear with VR support.

To conceptualize gamification features for a VR fitness product is a straightforward process. Due to the fact that most VR fitness products simulate real-life situations, it is necessary to study what gamification features and concepts have worked well in real life and transfer that knowledge into the simulated VR fitness world.

One example would be to study what a market leader such as Fitbit has done to become successful. Fitbit is a UX-driven company that is known to have nailed gamification. Transferring the Fitbit success formula to XR gamification would mean to apply the UX design process by identifying user pain points and solving the problems that are in the way of making a VR workout fun, enjoyable, and satisfying. Gamification helped Fitbit to make a workout competitive, social, and challenging enough to keep the user engaged while keeping the process simple enough. The companion app assists the user with a clean UI that makes it easy to check on progress, in addition to playful rewards and positive nudging for better accomplishments.

Most of the standard gamification features can be found in the leading VR cycling solutions by VirZOOM and Holodia. VR environments are an ideal playground for fitness gamification to increase motivation and user engagement through fun elements to distract from the potentially unpleasant and repetitive tasks of a workout.

Gamified XR fitness based on UX design solutions is in the forefront of a new industry that will shape personal fitness in the years to come. VR is expected to become a major force in the fitness industry, because it has the potential to solve a lot of the problems users face. The UX design process with a focus on gamification unleashes new opportunities that real-life fitness tracking apps don't even have. Being able to customize the immersive environment according to the user's persona, directing the user flow and delivering a bespoke experience that is targeting exactly what the user needs at that moment in time while analyzing and interpreting the user's motion data, improving feedback and results, is the long-term vision. It is no surprise that exercise-oriented VR apps such as Beat Saber and BOXVR are among the best-selling VR titles. Room-scale movement in VR is an obvious win for fun exercises, just like Nintendo's Wii Sports was an instant hit for the company, due to the fact that it included physical gameplay. Nintendo's Wii Sports success turned the Wii into a fitness gamification pioneer that has most likely inspired a lot of other sports games, including Sports Scramble on the Oculus Quest.

2.5.5 AR Gamification

Gamified AR applications have been a success story within their limited handheld niche. Once AR wearables become mainstream, they are expected to revolutionize marketing and retail. Turning a shopping routine into an immersive gamified experience offers a lot of benefits to brands. Trackable user engagement at the retail shelf, extending reward and loyalty systems to on-site interaction, and additional options for tryouts using AR mirrors and overlays have the potential to make a brand more engaging and emotional. AR gamification has the potential to bring a brand's stories to life in front of the user's eyes. The long-term benefits are better brand awareness, brand loyalty, and ultimately better sales. Gamification strategies that have been proven to work for web and mobile applications can be brought into the real world using an AR gamification layer embedded into the spatial presence of a brand.

Gamified AR is also reshaping the tourism and hospitality industries by using personalized, location-based marketing. AR-enhanced services like tour guides, personalized special offers on location and special rewards based on earned badges or trophies, immersive navigation assistance, and AR-enabled hotel features give the brand experience a competitive edge in a crowded market.

Besides marketing and retail, AR gamification shines when it comes to acquiring knowledge at locations with educational context. Historical sites, museums, and cultural heritage projects are able to benefit from a gamified AR approach that encourages user engagement, interest, and social interaction with the exhibits. Examples are map-based treasure hunts that serve as a semi-automated guide through a historic site, stimulating the user to complete a set of tokens, coins, or badges and to share the successful completion on social media.

Heritage experiences using AR gamification have been successfully used with handheld mobile devices. The approach has shown to stimulate public interest and the user engagement with the exhibit. Case studies have revealed that the UX design process was of essential importance in developing the application concept, though ideation, prototyping, and usability tests using focus groups. The experience and learnings from gamification using handheld AR will leverage the use cases of wearable AR, once it becomes widely available and affordable enough to enter the mass market. Game mechanics and use cases are very similar, except that wearable AR glasses enable a more persuasive experience, a fact that is expected to be a great accelerator for a better learning experience in the AR road map ahead.

2.6 Summary

This chapter looked at the history and future of the XR industry and its usability pain points, use cases, and reference titles. It looked at the core components for an XR experience, devices and application types, as well as experience categories and evaluated how mega trends in the digital economy will shape the future XR ecology. The chapter looked at best practices and heuristics for XR and examined the increasing importance of privacy UX in the face of the emerging AR cloud. Finally, it analyzed the role that UX plays as an activator for the XR paradigm shift and how the rise of gamification opened the door for better user engagement.

CHAPTER 3

The Rise of UX and How It Drives XR User Adoption

3.1 Introduction

This chapter is dedicated to the economic context of UX and XR. What does UX mean for the game industry, and how has the digital landscape changed that game engine toolsets and frameworks became more important for the success of digital XR products? What are the future-proof use cases and emerging standards from recent VR history, and what design philosophy is most relevant for the future role of XR designers?

3.2 UX and the Macroeconomics of the Next Big Thing

UX design is, to a great degree, a strategic business tool. While helping to solve the user's problem using technology, its purpose is, to the same degree, to succeed in its goals as a business and win over the user as a

© Cornel Hillmann 2021
C. Hillmann, *UX for XR*, https://doi.org/10.1007/978-1-4842-7020-2_3

customer. A popular diagram illustrates this point, in positioning UX in the central intersection between business and user (Figure 3-1).

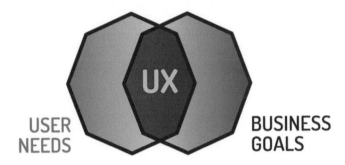

Figure 3-1. *Positioning UX (image by C. Hillmann)*

In the world of web and mobile application development, this formula has been the foremost success factor of the digital economy. Technological innovation has to solve user problems, and problem-solving has to be tied to a business model to enable growth. A thriving digital economy depends on growth to create long-term value by expansion. This ecology has been allowing businesses to improve products and services and ultimately improve value to the user over time while feeding back into technical innovation. UX is the centerpiece of an expanding ecosystem in the process of creating value.

This process is, of course, not only true for digital products, but for anything, digital or physical. Nevertheless, it is the digital and always connected economy that enables an environment for rapid growth. Digital globalization has been a catalyst for many ecommerce shooting stars and will continue to drive the rapid expansion of start-ups that take advantage of the cross-border opportunities in the digital age. The era of digital disruption that started in the 1990s is still in its early stages and will continue to revolutionize society, culture, and the economy. AR and VR are part of the process to create new growth opportunities and empower people, once the initial roadblocks are removed.

3.2.1 UX Designers and the Digital Economy

The success of the UX design process, its importance for the growth areas in the economy, and the enormous value it has created for successful and very often disruptive digital products have also opened up new opportunities for designers. UX designers are facing a growing demand from developers and, in addition, are enjoying a thriving ecosystem of new tools and services catering to the industry. In the long run, this trend is unlikely to change, as technological innovation needs UX designers to turn innovation into successful products. New technologies that are shaping the digital landscape of the future, be it XR, AI, IoT, or blockchain-related applications, will continue to drive product innovation with a need to conceptualize and optimize the user's interaction.

While the industry-specific UX process may get refined over the years and the tools may become more convenient and powerful, its core fundamentals will most likely remain consistent: to empathize with the user and research, ideate, prototype, test, and implement solutions (Figure 3-2).

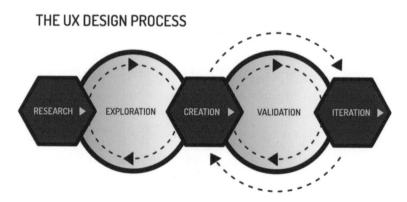

THE UX DESIGN PROCESS

RESEARCH ▶   EXPLORATION   CREATION ▶   VALIDATION   ITERATION ▶

Figure 3-2. *The design process (image by C. Hillmann)*

The user experience is where businesses fail or succeed. No matter how amazing the technology or how visionary the company's strategy, if it doesn't win over the user, a product may fail or lose out to the competition. UX is where all efforts are judged by the user. To win over the user, more than usability is needed. Desirability is the factor that makes users return to the product, because it creates long-lasting value and has a meaningful and satisfying effect on the users (Figure 3-3).

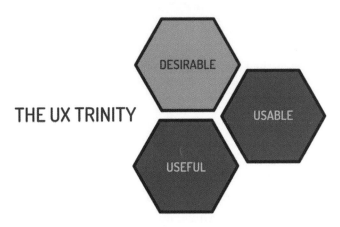

Figure 3-3. *UX, usability, and desirability (image by C. Hillmann)*

For example, successful fintech, fitness, or photo-sharing apps have in common that they provide a solution that is perceived as not only valuable but also affects the user on an emotional level. For XR products to succeed, the same standards apply. The product has to offer a solution for a problem, in such a satisfying way that an emotional connection is established and the user happily returns to it.

A number of design-driven XR applications for HMDs have succeeded with emotional design, but are facing other hurdles on the road to success. The limited distribution reach for XR apps is often a problem, even if the business proposal is revolutionary, the UX design is exceptional, and an innovative solution to user problems has been established. Distribution scope to obtain a critical mass, necessary for start-up funding and a healthy growth environment, is a factor that is expected to develop over time.

3.2.2 Macrotechnology Forces

The potential of VR and AR products in the larger economy is enormous, and numerous studies have proven the benefits of AR and VR in education, training, and ecommerce.

What is holding the industry back, considering its niche market share? It is pretty obvious that the limited distribution and availability of XR headsets is the prime reason, next to high cost, technical restrictions, and lack of awareness. Luckily, these pain points are temporary problems and are expected to be resolved over the next few years, according to most surveys. "Widespread consumer adoption of XR headsets is not expected to take off until at least 2023," reported SuperData, a leading provider of market intelligence, in a Q3 2020 update. Until that point in time is reached, where headsets are a part of almost every household, the classic chicken and egg dilemma continues to exist: To attract a mass audience, "must-have" social applications are needed, but for them to work, an infrastructure of widely available headsets is required. A good example are VR meeting apps that have been proven to be superior over videoconferencing in a number of ways. Virtual meetings in VR are better in communicating nonverbal cues, and the brain tends to retain information much better through muscle memory and the contextual, spatial experience than from the typical grid of video streams in a video conference call, where people often struggle with audio and video connection issues.

The benefits of VR meetups are enormous, but the technology still fails to scale due to the lack of headset availability. For regular team meetups within a corporate structure, this can be arranged with prior planning, while the chances to switch to VR on any private call are rare, due to the lack of market penetration that XR has at its current state.

Despite their proven value, the full potential of XR technologies remains largely untapped at this point. Viewing the development in the context of the macro trends of the digital age, it is no question that, as XR capabilities mature, the content offering expands, and the adoption rates increase, the critical mass of market penetration will gradually materialize to finally energize a flourishing platform for entrepreneurs, developers, and UX designers.

Funding via seed investment and venture capital typically increases exponentially once development accelerates due to rapid-fire innovation and adoption at the critical stages. The digital economy continues to be driven by hungry investors in search of a growth story. The long-term economic environment, including the outlook for monetary policies based on low interest rates, serves as an accelerator for this trend.

The economic environment and its dynamics and business goals are part of the underlying forces that UX design is facing. The UX stage is the final test for a product and its business concept; therefore, the stakes are high, and the importance of the UX design process is increasingly critical for adoption rates of innovative solutions based on new technology.

3.2.3 How Free-to-Play Games Disrupted the Gaming Industry

A good example of how a macro trend turned an industry upside down and UX entered the stage is the game industry. It was not too long ago, up until about 2010, that a game would typically be purchased at a retail outlet, for example, a GameStop branch. A game was considered a software entertainment product that would sit on the retail shelf until it found a new owner. A finished product that was advertised and sold like any other retail stock item. UX played only a minor role in the interaction between the title and the user. The interaction between product and user was simple; if the product didn't deliver on its promises, the user would most likely not buy another title from the same developer.

Soon after 2010, digital distribution and mobile and social gaming revolutionized important sections of the game industry, and its business model was forced to transform into an entirely different revenue strategy. What started with Zynga's game FarmVille and its in-game currency of *farm coins* as a revenue stream soon led to numerous counterparts in other gaming genres, up to the overwhelming success of Fortnite, introduced in 2017. Fortnite became the most influential game of the decade, with a revenue of US\$ 1.8 billion in 2019 and over 350 million registered players in 2020. As a battle royale game, Fortnite is free to play (F2P), but offers in-game purchases to enhance the player experience. The F2P model was not entirely new; it had in previous decades been used with *massive multiplayer online games* (MMOG), especially by the Korean and Russian gaming communities. The 2010s brought the concept to a wider global audience, due to the availability of fast Internet connections and the increasing acceptance of online transactions.

Once online transactions became important in gaming, so did UX design. The UX design process was geared toward the conversion of F2P players into paying customers. Very soon, the UX design process established itself as a new and powerful force next to game design.

3.2.4 The Culture Clash: UX Design vs. Game Design

As pointed out in the introduction to this book, the rise of UX design for game development is very relevant for XR. The original production environment for XR content is game development. XR applications are built with game engines, and their processes follow game development standards and conventions.

The success of UX design in the digital economy is built on web and mobile app development. UX design, especially the branch geared toward UI, UX/UI design, comes from a different design culture. Both approach the design of a digital product from a different angle. Game design is focused on the overall success of an entertainment software product that is able to entertain the user, while UX design is taking a player-centric and often conversion-oriented approach to improve the gameplay experience by leveraging psychology and behavioral science.

Both approaches have a lot of areas in common; the game designer cares just as much as the UX designer for the overall user experience, the game mechanics, rewards, storytelling, and ultimately player retention. Game design is successful if the user has a positive, meaningful, and satisfying experience.

With the rise of F2P games, the role of the game designer changed dramatically. The new business model of free games with in-game purchases forced game publishers to focus on the short-term retention of first-time players. Players need to be teased and engaged early on in the game, to create attachment to the title by making the first in-game purchase. This is a strategy that is essential to the business model, as a free game is quickly populated with a lot of users, but only a tiny percentage is willing to actually spend money. Consequently, the game designer's role had shifted from the overall entertainment value of the product toward the conversion during the first contact. The conversion rate, of users taking a desired action, in this case making an in-game purchase, became the essential metric that determined the success of a game. The conversion event as a key performance indicator (KPI) for ecommerce applications plays a vital role in measuring the return on investment (ROI) of UX design. The rise and success of the UX design process metrics in the digital economy that had powered the success stories of web and mobile apps became important metrics for game design. A sharp focus of UX design on player psychology, behavioral patterns, early gratifications, and frictionless onboarding became the essential part of the F2P monetization business model. As a result, the game designer's role has shifted to include more UX responsibilities. This trend has since moved to other game types beyond F2P, giving more importance to ergonomics, interface, and frictionless onboarding.

UX designers in turn had to expand their skills in the area of game design, as gamification became more important for web and mobile applications and UX for games gained traction. The result is that game design and UX design overlap to a certain degree. As both design approaches move into each other's territory, there is also a potential for conflict. Most of the time they are perceived as complementary: game design with a focus on content creation and UX design for tweaking the user interaction. Traditionally, the game designer's responsibility is that of an author and world creator, while the UX designer on a game focuses on removing friction and improving the user experience by helping to discover and understand the content. UX design can help to apply methods to existing content as opposed to the wider responsibilities of the game designer that include content creation. But the takeaway now is this: Both professions can overlap each other, certain UX design principles can live in the game design world, and vice versa.

3.2.5 Conversion Events

UX design has become important for microtransaction in F2P games. The conversion rate is the metric to verify how well the UX design performs, very often analyzed with A/B tests. The very performance-oriented design method is occasionally viewed with skepticism by veteran game designers, when discussing priorities of a digital game product. The quality of the content has to have at least the same priority as the conversion road map, when defining the product's long-term goals.

In-app purchases and ecommerce transactions are only one variety of a conversion event. The definition of conversion goes well beyond a commercial purchase and can be any key performance indicator (KPI) that has been defined as an important goal for the project. Conversion events can be as follows: a specific learning outcome, a minimum of time spent using the application, filling out a form, signing up for membership or a mailing list, or any a call to action (Figure 3-4).

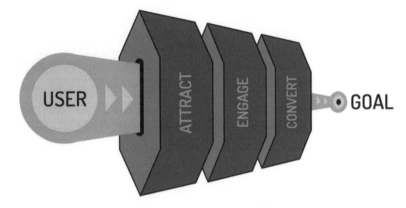

Figure 3-4. *UX and conversion (image by C. Hillmann)*

Only a small percentage of the AR and VR market is currently driven by in-app purchases or classic conversion events; therefore, a stronger UX focus is mostly on the overall success of the experience, where the conversion events are often focused on returning users and retention during gameplay. Anything that can be measured has the potential to be a conversion event.

Optimizing conversion through usability and desirability, using established UX methods, is a way to improve the quality and user satisfaction of a digital XR product and is at this stage of the XR ecology, most often, a priority over direct monetization.

3.2.6 From Human-Centered Design to the Human-Centered Economy

The economic context and the role that UX design plays for the success stories in the digital economy have occasionally led to misconceptions. Critical voices have, in rare cases, labeled UX design as manipulative, due to the fact that human psychology and behavior patterns are used to generate sales.

An increasing awareness and ongoing debate over "dark pattern" UX design that is intended to mislead and trick the user has contributed to the notion, even though they contradict the ethical code of design guidelines. As much as UX techniques can be abused by bad actors in the industry, they can contribute to good causes.

UX design is an optimization process and, in the wider sense, much more than its typical application in the digital economy. It is important to recognize that profitability is only one of many ways that UX design can play out. If the conversion event of a set goal is in a nonprofit context, then UX design helps to maximize the effort, by finding the most efficient way to communicate it to the user. UX design goals and conversion events are just as useful for applications where monetization is not the priority, such as XR experiences for learning and training.

Even though UX design has emerged as a powerhouse in respect to the financial success of digital products with a commercial goal, it remains just as powerful in areas where the goals are humanitarian and for the good of society, without monetization as the primary objective. UX design is a method of creating and optimizing the interaction with a design, to the benefit of the user. A positive and meaningful experience can be part of a commercial goal as well as the desired outcome for an experience that is part of a nonprofit campaign.

While UX design is typically associated with economic success, it can also be seen in the context of human-centered design (HCD). The latter, as an overarching framework in close relationship with design thinking, is regarded as a principal way for product design in general.

In contrast to the very narrow commercial interpretation of UX design, efforts have been made to take the idea into the opposite direction of seeing its progress as part of a move toward a human-centered economy.

The human-centered economy can be seen as an idea that emerged from think tanks and policy and research institutes advocating economic reforms to put human interests before corporate values. It can be seen in a wider context of the model of participatory economics, where the policy focus is on diminishing inequality and the negative side effects of destructive economic growth, targeting climate change, degrowth, and the circular economy.

Using this point of view, UX and human-centered design can be interpreted from a completely different angle, instead of being only product design oriented; it extends the larger context from a user-centric approach to a human-centric philosophy. The benefit of this point of view is that seeing UX design in the context of humanitarian goals gives the role of the UX designer a greater sense of purpose, especially when future technology and its use are critical for the benefit of society.

The UX of human-centric design approaches can take on a different meaning, depending on the context and objective, for example, when considering environment-centered design (ECD) whereby the human is the center of the hierarchy, but socially and economically sustainable factors are part of the holistic thinking.

The wide field of design thinking demonstrates that beginning with conversion-driven UX techniques for ecommerce up to methodological thinking on how to improve the framework for the society of the future, it is dependent on the goal and mission and in what context UX techniques are applied.

Immersive AR and VR applications cover a lot of areas that are critical to the success of society in general, putting user empathy first, making privacy and data security a priority, therefore advocating human/user value as the ultimate goal, by putting persons before system efficiency as a core value.

3.2.7 Economic Success as an Accelerator

The economic success of UX design in the digital economy has been an accelerator for the recognition of its principles, methods, and techniques. The side effect of the commercial success and the wealth it has generated is that other areas are benefiting along with it. The growth of UX research, its tools, and support organizations are available to develop

XR interactions further, using the same approach that has built the digital economy around web and mobile apps. This vast knowledge and experience is making it easier for the next generation of XR applications to succeed, even outside of the commercial realm. The business aspect of UX design, the economic environment, and the long-term technological trends, including business opportunities, have been shaping UX methods and tools, to a degree that it is benefiting any sectors where design is important.

Borrowing from commercial UX to use the same design principles, methods, and techniques for nonprofit, educational, CivicTech, or GovTech products means using a powerful toolset that has proven itself in a highly competitive market environment for philanthropic or idealistic projects.

3.3 Key Lessons from Three Decades of VR Experiences

At the beginning of the 1990s, the VR pioneer VPL Research went out of business, leaving behind a legacy of innovation and patents that were snatched up by Sun Microsystems. Sun was a computer company specialized in graphics workstations, which, like Silicon Graphics, Inc., also known as SGI, helped to revolutionize 3D graphics and its use in entertainment products.

Even though VPL went out of business, it became obvious that simulated 3D worlds had a strong attraction for the entertainment industry. The idea to bring never-seen-before images to life, and possibly even step inside such a world, was immediately seen as a potential growth area for film and interactive entertainment products.

3.3.1 1990s VR: The Public Is Ready, the Technology Is Not

Artificial worlds, sci-fi adventures, and fantasy destinations generated by computer graphics were the entertainment promise, fueled by pop culture expectations. Nevertheless, the technology was not ready for the futuristic ideas of early innovators and enthusiasts. The learning from that early phase is that the demand for VR is real. It is not an artificial concept that is pushed on consumers by corporations; instead, it has deep roots in art, literature, mythology, and pop culture, including its various subculture genres and niches.

But, to bring the technology to a level where a consumer-friendly experience is actually possible, it took around three decades. Early VR gave a tiny taste of the things to come, but to make a valuable, meaningful, and enjoyable experience available on affordable hardware was a major evolution, where the UX perspective played a major role at the later stages. Part of the evolution was enabled by the availability of game engines that allowed the prototyping, testing, and unification of all technical elements required to deliver a convincing product. Let's not forget that before Unity and Unreal, game engines were mostly coded in-house. Individual developers had to assemble middleware solutions for physics simulation, AI, sound, GUI, and so on, to bring all the complex components together. A coding-intensive pipeline that made 3D ideation and rapid prototypes difficult and not a very UX design–friendly environment, due to the fact that it was difficult to quickly adopt changes based on playtest results and tweak user flow, resulting from feedback, in an agile design sprint. The coding bottleneck for entertainment software development has been very obvious for a complex product as a 3D game where a long list of specialized software had to be integrated to enable the basic feature set.

3.3.2 The Visual Scripting Evolution: From Virtools to Blueprints and Bolt

Thankfully, software development for 3D real-time applications saw a new trend emerging: visual scripting. The company Virtools, founded in 1993, targeting mostly industrial and enterprise system integrators, was one of the first commercial applications to allow editing object parameters and behaviors with a visual flowchart in an interactive 3D real-time engine. The Virtools Scripting Language (VSL) gave nonprogrammers the tools to quickly edit the interactions, allowing to prototype user interaction. When the Unreal Engine 3 was introduced in 2004, it paved the way for Kismet, the visual scripting language that was created to allow level editors to prototype gameplay, with a visual node-based system. Kismet paved the way for Unreal Engine 4's (UE4) powerful visual scripting system Blueprints, which is a complete node-based gameplay scripting system with deep engine integration.

Visual coding made it possible for designers to use the full range of tools previously only available to programmers. It empowered the designer to quickly create and test interactions, an important step for the UX design process at the prototyping stage (Figure 3-5).

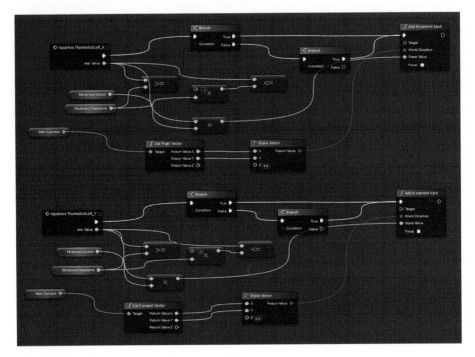

Figure 3-5. *Visual scripting tools: UE4 Blueprints*

Users of the competing engine Unity had for the longest time used the plugin Playmaker, among others, as a visual programming solution to test and prototype user interactions and game logic. Playmaker is a state machine and had limitations when it came to more complex gameplay. The introduction of the Unity plugin Bolt offered an alternative on the same level as Blueprints for Unreal. On May 4, 2020, Unity Technologies acquired the solution from the developer Ludiq. The fact that the visual scripting solution Bolt is becoming a core technology for the Unity engine is important for UX designers looking for a tool to prototype AR and VR user interfaces, interactions, and game mechanics without having to touch any code. Both the Unreal and the Unity engine have developed into designer-friendly environments that allow testing, ideation, and prototyping as part of the UX design process, instead of having to depend on programmers, which very often is the development bottleneck of a production. Coding for designers has become a reality through visual scripting solutions. Together with frameworks and sector-specific toolsets, they provide the essential and accessible elements to build, prototype, and test user interactions. Tweaking the user experiences, by optimizing the user interaction, based on ideation, concepts, and testing, is such an essential part of the UX design process that visual scripting opens up important opportunities for UX designers who prefer to be hands-on, by allowing access to design parameters that were previously only accessible on the coding level, including tools to monitor and measure user behavior. The evolution that led to Blueprints in Unreal and Bolt in Unity is an essential step in empowering UX designers, not only to access game and UI logic but also to be deeply involved through the full project lifecycle.

3.3.3 VR Solutions with Staying Power

VR hardware and software have matured over the last three decades, making commercial product development viable for pioneering entrepreneurs. The previous decades had seen mostly simple games and industrial application for 3D product visualization, while the full potential of VR was still considered unmapped territory. With the introduction of the new VR generation since 2013 and the explosion of experimental, commercial, and education titles, the experience of more than seven years using the robust toolsets of commercial game engines allows us to analyze where VR contributed to solutions that had staying power and a future potential. From the UX design perspective, that means solving user problems with VR and evaluating the minimum viable product (MVP) examples in the VR space. Whenever VR accomplishes to create value beyond the novelty factor for real-life problems for consumers and professionals beyond tech enthusiasts, a long-term growth potential is very likely. Let's have a look at some areas where VR has proven to be successful and the degree to which UX design can play a role in bringing it to the next level.

Consumer:

- Immersive gaming

- Immersive media

- Social VR

Enterprise:

- Product visualization and development

- VR co-working, productivity, team meetings

Retail:

- Product tryouts, demonstrations, and explainers

- VR brand experiences

Medical:

- Patient communication

- Rehab, antianxiety applications

Education:

- Educational experiences

- Simulation and training

Immersive gaming:

Immersive gaming has been the driving force behind the Oculus success story. Co-founder Palmer Luckey was a modding enthusiast, and his VR vision was in line with what that community expected from a VR future: the next level of immersive gaming to replace extensive gaming rigs with multiple monitors. Immersive gaming is an obvious and proven use case.

The advantage: Being part of the game world, experiencing the scale of it, and interacting with body and hand movements, making interaction more fun and intuitive.

Immersive media:

Immersive media has outgrown its novelty phase and is now a solid VR staple. Commercial VR video transitioned its format preference from nonstereoscopic 360-degree to stereoscopic VR180 video. The reason: VR180 covers higher pixel density in the front-facing field of view. The stereoscopic image of VR180 video is especially ideal for performances such as concerts, theater, or stand-up comedy. Often, the performance venue concept is split into the front-facing VR video space and the back-facing auditorium using polygon geometry. This solution, part linear VR video, part interactive geometry, offers the best of both worlds.

Animation in VR has carved out its own niche, driven by the unique storytelling benefits that immersive animation has to offer. The Oculus application Quill delivers a lineup of unique storytelling tools to let the user experience the magic of living dioramas through the VR looking glass. To follow characters and their story in a hand-drawn environment is a powerful and unique way to evoke emotions. The immersive intimacy and creative freedom is seen as the future of art and design by its many evangelists. For UX designers, it is a sandbox for ideas and an opportunity for spatial experimentation.

Social VR:

Social VR has been an important part of Oculus' road map since it became part of Facebook and its stated mission to connect people around the world. The original social space, Oculus Rooms, has been replaced with Oculus Horizon, a multiuser sandbox creation space. Similar social meeting spaces, such as Rec Room and Altspace, have been growing their user base with VR activities and social events.

While Rec Room has been popular with a younger teenage audience, AltspaceVR has been the social VR go-to place for adults. Founded in 2013, AltspaceVR is one of the long-term survivors of VR, pioneering the social VR space, and was bought over by Microsoft in 2017, at a time of crisis, when the future of AltspaceVR was in doubt due to the lack of funding. The company has been pioneering regular community events and VR meetups with a focus on real value to its users. Another popular social application, Bigscreen VR, had success with social viewing, a concept of sharing a screen with friends. Social VR for consumers has received more attention as a result of the worldwide Covid-19 pandemic (and subsequent lockdowns preventing real-world interactions), and it is expected to be a key driver for the long-term success of VR.

Enterprise VR:

Enterprise VR has become a natural extension of the product visualization process, where CAD/CAM data is fed into a real-time graphics engine such as Unreal and using the datasmith pipeline, as an example. Enterprise VR has had a place in product design and manufacturing before the current VR wave. It has pioneered VR for simulation and product design purposes and will accelerate its growth in that sector. The new generation of VR tech makes enterprise VR attractive for smaller businesses, including design studios, where pre-visualization is part of the value chain. Another area where VR has had proven success is in training. Typical examples are staff training on pre-visualized machinery or sites. This approach serves as a substantial time and cost saver, due to the fact that downtime to train staff on new equipment or at a new site can be reduced to a minimum. In other areas, corporate training, virtual meetings, and VR presentations have taken off since the pandemic forced companies to rethink their communication strategies.

VR in retail:

VR has been a proven tool in the retail space, when the product is based on a unique experience speaking to all senses. Luxury car makers or real estate developers have offered VR introductions to their products as an extension of their media presentation. Premium brands often use VR to introduce potential customers to new concepts in a playful way, not only at trade shows but also at dedicated in-store experience areas. Examples range from VR wine tastings to in-store VR product exploration, where VR helps to engage with the brand.

VR in healthcare:

VR has been a success story in healthcare, foremost for medical training to simulate surgical procedures, for example. Companies like ImmersiveTouch and Osso VR have successfully developed VR solutions to make healthcare training more efficient. Other VR healthcare use cases include using VR HMDs for distraction and relaxation, targeting patients suffering from anxieties during a medical procedure, and VR apps to help with rehab to support physical therapy.

VR in education:

VR in education has been popular in schools, such as using it for VR field trips to explore and experience historical sites. Google pioneered the concept with the Google Expeditions project in 2015. Since then, companies such as ThingLink have developed the concept of the immersive classroom further, providing a technology platform to engage students and optimize the learning process, especially when it comes to distant learning.

3.3.4 Emerging VR Conventions

In the previous chapter, we have established that groundbreaking titles, such as Half-Life: Alyx, set the bar for VR usability, due to Valve Corporation's extensive research in making the game as accessible as possible, by offering customization options for VR interaction. Beyond the core set of VR usability components, there are additional layers of UX conventions for VR experiences that are building up over time. Some of these conventions may change as the technology progresses. A lot of interactions, such as hand tracking, have the final goal to be as natural as real-world interactions. The vision is that a simulation would come as close as possible to the real thing. In terms of UX affordance, that means a virtual switch behaves as its real counterpart: One flips the finger over it to activate it, just as in the real world. Affordances bridge the gap between the digital and the real world. But, in addition to affordances, we also have VR conventions that help the user to avoid unpleasant experiences or to enhance the interaction, to make it more satisfying and meaningful. Interactions should, at a minimum, be comfortable and effortless, using familiar interactions like grab, pull, or push. Besides the goal of simulating reality, we also have the goal to provide shortcuts or superpowers where simulated reality could be too slow, cumbersome, or unresponsive. In that sense, reality simulation is not the only goal; instead, it is one of the goals next to explorability and enhanced interactive immersiveness to empower the user. To reach these goals, we use conventions that have been proven to work in that process (Figure 3-6).

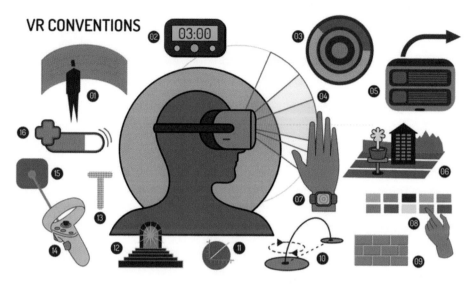

Figure 3-6. *VR conventions (image by C. Hillmann), clockwise: (01) curved screens; (02) diegetic UI; (03) long-press buttons; (04) comfort zones; (05) throwaway menu; (06) stereoscopic consistency; (07) the VR smartwatch; (08) hand interaction; (09) normal maps; (10) locomotion, rotation, options; (11) constant velocity; (12) VR onboarding; (13) text readability; (14) VR button conventions; (15) selection ray functions; (16) HUD motion lag*

VR conventions are fluid and priorities can change over time, as consumers adapt to VR. A good example is the subject of motion sickness that used to be the priority for VR onboarding and has now moved to lesser importance as more people have awareness of it and the majority of active users have developed "VR legs."

Some of the emerging VR conventions are described in the following:

Curved screens (01):

For very large menu screens in VR, typically used in launch or lobby environments, curved screens have been established to guarantee a continuous and comfortable viewing distance to the displayed information. The rule of thumb is the larger the screen, the more reason to have it curved. If the viewing distance to the far sections of a large flat menu results in distorted, hard-to-read text, a curved screen will fix that problem. An alternative is to have multiple flat screens, or flat screen sections arranged in a circular order, to maximize a consistent and user-friendly interaction experience.

Diegetic UI first (02):

Diegetic elements are considered to be part of the 3D game world. They fit in with the storytelling and visual style of the experience as opposed to head-up-display (HUD) UI elements that overlay the screen. Diegetic UI lives in the VR world and should be considered first when creating UI elements, as long as they make sense in the context of the application's goals. Examples of diegetic UI elements are the previously mentioned VR smartwatch, an actual watch on a desk as a timer, a LED display area on a gun showing the ammunition amount, and a tablet for inventory selections. Diegetic UI uses 3D objects that are part of the game world and storytelling to convey information as closely associated with their analogy in reality. For that reason, it makes the information more intuitive and integrated and should in most cases be preferred over non-diegetic, spatial-only, or meta UI options.

Long-press buttons (03):

Buttons with a circular progress bar allow the user to cancel an action in progress. This is a helpful function when activating a new level, launching a new experience, or initializing a dramatic change of the game environment that may take an extra effort to reverse.

Fuse buttons, first used with gaze in the early generation of low-end VR headsets, such as the Google Cardboard, made it possible to activate items by time-out using gaze aiming or in newer headsets by trigger activation with the controller selection ray (see Legacy interaction—gaze activation at the end of the section). A button will trigger with a time-out, by loading a radial progress bar while being activated, thus giving the user the option to cancel before committing. Due to the immersive nature of VR, dramatic changes in the environment have much higher visceral impact on the user, than in any other medium. The long-press button is therefore an essential VR convention to guard the user against decision mistakes and allows the user to recover from errors as defined in the ten usability heuristics for UI design by Jakob Nielsen. Typical examples are the large activation buttons in the Oculus games Sports Scramble and Dead and Buried II.

Comfort zones (04):

VR users are most comfortable when the interactive content is centered in a 70-degree left and right horizontal and 40-degree up and down vertical zone. Neck strain, posture, and a comfortable controller action space have to be considered for longer experiences. Interfaces too far up or down in the field of view and secondary action outside of the horizontal visual sweet spot should be avoided for longer periods, unless they are required by storytelling or are an essential part of the game's mechanics or story progression.

The throwaway—delete—gesture (05):

VR apps that allow the user to place objects or menus into the open 3D space need an easy way to reverse the action and delete it. The throwaway gesture—defined by grabbing the item and throwing it away—has been established as an intuitive method by a number of VR titles. The high-velocity arm swing and object release feels natural and adds a playful element that is intuitive, satisfying, and easy to remember by the user. Creative VR apps such as Tilt Brush and Gravity Sketch are examples in which the user, by throwing the object off screen, can get rid of parked menus that populate the 3D environment.

Stereoscopic consistency (06):

Stereo perception tapers off at about 20 meters. To deliver the most satisfying 3D viewing experience, consistent elements in the fore-, middle-, and background should be maintained when possible. Background: More than 20 meters away. Middle ground: 5–15 meters away. Foreground: Items less than 5 meters away. Designing the perceived depth and spatial layout of an experience by considering the three zones approach helps to keep the user interested and engaged.

The VR smartwatch menu (07):

Accessing a user menu by activating a virtual smartwatch, typically on the user's left arm in VR, has established itself as an often-used intuitive convention for VR menus. Very often, the smartwatch is just an access point to serve discoverability with a visual reminder. The selection ray activation is most often followed by a radial pop-up menu, a concept that can easily carry over to AR. As a convenient item that is consistently in the same place, even as the environment changes, the VR smartwatch has occasionally been expanded to the full arm or even both arms for different menu sections.

Hand interaction (08):

As an alternative to controller-based VR interaction, hand tracking is becoming an intuitive solution for VR experiences where hand poses and gestures feel more natural as an input. The Oculus hand tracking SDK provides a solid toolkit for developers to get started. Hand tracking can, for example, be an alternative when targeting a casual user who is not familiar with gaming controllers or when input with multiple fingers makes sense, for example, with virtual keyboards and instruments. The MRTK framework, one of the most intuitive and sophisticated hand interaction frameworks used with the HoloLens 2, has been ported to Oculus VR. This will help UX/UI designers to keep XR continuity across VR and AR applications.

Hand tracking is a work in progress. The challenge of hand tracking is the lack of precision and haptic feedback that controllers can provide. The following is one rule-of-thumb list for hand interaction:

a) Create affordances for 3D objects that require hand interaction.

b) Use audio-visual signifiers and feedback to assist in the interaction (shadows and glow for proximity, sound for activation, and animation triggers).

Button size, position, and comfortable proximity are important aspects for button and interactive object usability using hand tracking. Initiation and completion state should always be clearly visible.

Normal maps (09):

For 3D computer graphics and especially traditional game texture mapping, normal mapping is an essential technique to add surface detail without additional geometry. Normal maps give the illusion of 3D detail. In VR, normal mapping has limits, because the normal map 3D illusion does not work with stereoscopic perception. Nevertheless, it still works for fine detail when interacting with light sources. To ensure normal maps work in VR, designers have to make sure the following:

a) That only small surface details are expressed through normal maps, while medium and larger surface details are better implemented through actual polygon geometry to look natural.

b) That the viewing angle and viewing distance to normal maps are designed in a way to not reveal the "fake" 3D nature of the normal map. Objects that are viewed at close distance should not depend on normal maps as well as surface areas exposed to extreme viewing angles.

Using normal maps used to be a taboo in the earlier days of VR, but the attitude toward them has changed over time. An increasing number of VR titles have shown that normal maps work well in VR, if done right. Normal maps are now a standard ingredient of 3D graphics for contemporary VR environments, but have to be handled with care to be convincing.

Locomotion, snap rotation, motion sickness options (10):

As mentioned in the previous chapter, VR usability standards are set by such milestone titles as Half-Life: Alyx. Part of the success of AAA VR titles is the extensive research that a large developer, such as Valve Corporation, is able to invest into UX fundamentals, to make sure the game is as accessible as possible. The gold standard that titles such as Half Life: Alyx have established is as follows: Give users locomotion options covering teleportation to smooth locomotion, allow users to adjust the snap rotation type and angle, and offer options to ease motion sickness, if required, next to accessibility, left/right, one-handed, and seated/standing options.

Next to the standard options, there is one approach to manage motion sickness that has become less used in recent years, but is occasionally still available in the user game-setting options, the so-called "comfort vignette": a technique to temporarily narrow down the field of view during any kind of movement.

Constant velocity (11):

To avoid motion sickness for "on-rails" experiences, where the user moves from hotspot to hotspot along a predefined path, constant velocity helps to keep motion sickness at check for sensible users. Changing velocity, acceleration, and deceleration are natural in the real world, but can have unwanted side effects when experienced in VR, unless the target audience is expecting it, such as in a roller-coaster simulation.

VR onboarding (12):

What happens during the first minute of a VR experience is extremely important. The first-time user experience (FTUE) in traditional UX design is typically counted in seconds. In VR we have to give a bit more leeway, as loading times are longer and a larger viewing space requires more time for adjustment. Nevertheless, the principles are the same. A great FTUE helps the user by reducing the cognitive load and minimizing the effort to learn about the basics of the product, by helping to orient and interact using a clear design structure. Using a familiar design language with common patterns typically helps in this process. Removing barriers, by communicating the basic functions and button mappings, using skippable tutorials in addition to visual teasers of the content to expect, ensures the user feels comfortable enough to come back and thus keeps retention rates high.

Text readability (13):

Issues around text readability have plagued VR experiences since the beginning. Anti-aliasing problems and flicker are among the typical concerns that are caused by compression errors, technical limitations, and low-resolution HMD displays. Parts of the problem will resolve once higher-resolution VR displays are more common. Especially small typography is often hard to read in VR and often distorted by perspective due to different viewing angles. Common solutions are these: Avoid small text and make sure that fonts used are not too light, as well as arrange menus and text areas to face the user, and use a contrasting background and a minimum viewing distance.

VR button conventions (14):

As application functions vary, so do VR controller button assignments. Nevertheless, two buttons are consistent with most applications: the grip button to grab and the trigger button to activate. When designing for a genre or specific type of application, it makes sense to research the conventions of sector and application type. For example, Gravity Sketch, Tilt Brush, and Quill use the grip buttons to scale items with both controllers. Therefore, it would make sense to follow these conventions for any scale action in a creative VR application, reducing the cognitive load for the user.

Selection ray functions (15):

The motion controller selection ray is a standard that spans from simple 3DOF to high-end 6DOF headsets. It is the standard way of interacting with the environment, to move and interact with scene objects, including menus and UI functions. VR users typically expect visual and/or haptic feedback when interacting with a virtual object. These are typically object highlight, object outline highlight, and controller vibration. To pull in a selected object, the analog stick is often used to move the object along the selection ray, as an alternative to the gravity pull gesture featured in Half-Life: Alyx.

HUD motion lag (16):

VR experience designs that require a HUD or dashboard that is continuously showing have to face the difficult decision of where to position it without irritating the user (upper third for downward-oriented action, lower third for upward-oriented action). Continuous HUDs in VR can feel intrusive and unnatural. One design solution to make the HUD feel more organic is to give it a slight motion lag. When in use, the motion lag simulates the physical behavior of actual wearables by their weight and is therefore more easily accepted by the user.

VR menus:

The traditional pull-down or dropdown menus of desktop apps don't work well in VR; instead, radial menus have established themselves as one of the new standards for contextual menus. Radial menus are intuitive, user-friendly, and aesthetically pleasing and can be expanded to a great degree.

Another emerging standard is the 3D menu, which allows the user to flip the sides of a geometric object, locked to a controller, in order to access different menu panels. Google's Tilt Brush application for VR sketching is an example of how intuitive this concept is in making a number of menu panels easily accessible in VR and thus increasing productivity. The Mixed Reality Toolkit (MRTK) of the HoloLens 2 has been made available on the Oculus platform and can be considered a leading design standard for intuitive UI interaction, using 3D menus, as well as a large variety of UI and input interaction types, by using hand tracking.

Legacy interaction—gaze activation:

Gaze activation used to be very popular with the very first mobile VR generation (such as Google Cardboard and Samsung Gear VR) and should be mentioned here as well. The reason for its widespread use was its simplicity: No controller action was needed for interaction, as the center-view reticle, often in the form of a crosshair, would activate once the raycast hit an interactive item. A timer, mostly presented as a circular load bar around the crosshair, was used to confirm the action, leaving the user enough time to cancel by looking away before timeout. This input method has almost completely disappeared, as most activation and interaction is now handled by VR controllers. Nevertheless, gaze activation is occasionally used for its simplicity in object or menu interaction, and it had a comeback with VR fitness applications, especially when the controllers are tied to a workout machine and are unavailable for interface interaction.

3.3.5 The Shifting Landscape of VR

VR conventions change over time. Back in 2016, the focus was on motion sickness prevention and presence, the feeling of being there in VR. Teleportation was considered the only appropriate method of locomotion in VR, and it was considered wrong to use normal maps to depict surface detail for a VR experience. Fast forward to 2021 and these conventions have completely changed. Motion sickness issues are dealt with in a more subtle and proactive way. Hardly anyone speaks about presence anymore, as the novelty of the buzzword has worn off; instead, the feeling of VR presence is taken for granted. Smooth locomotion has been added as an alternative to teleportation to the users' options, where it makes sense, and fine-detail normal maps are basically part of any VR experience that is trying to achieve a higher degree of surface realism.

The problem of rapidly changing conventions is that guidelines and course materials for aspiring XR designers become quickly outdated. Very often, the change of conventions is led by popular games or spearheading applications that get quickly adopted by other developers, while the published material can lag a few years behind. For that reason, UX designers in the XR field have to constantly research all current design trends and observe the constantly changing user preferences. A good example was the move to smooth locomotion due to pressure from users. While most guidelines were teaching to use only teleportation, the reality was that most applications had already moved on to giving the user a smooth locomotion option, to keep all user types happy. Only developers and XR designers unaware of the change from using outdated reference materials would insist on offering only teleportation. The design space for VR interactions has matured over the years and is now looking beyond VR platforms at the bigger picture of XR standards. One example is the previously mentioned Mixed Reality Toolkit (MRTK) for the HoloLens 2, which has established itself as a leading AR framework for hand interactions. MRTK is now available for both AR and VR hand interactions and thus demonstrates how XR standards can work across platforms.

The three decades of VR experimentation and development behind us have gone through three important stages: at first, discovery and exploration of its potential; at the second stage, scientific application and usability refinement; and at its current (and third) stage, the push to a wider commercial market, where the technology is establishing itself in enterprise and consumer solutions, based on its 30-plus-year history.

3.4 XR Design: User Agency and Storytelling

The MRTK example illustrated the importance of frameworks for UX designers in the XR field. By choosing a platform, an engine, a framework, and a visual scripting language, XR designers make a decision on the toolset to craft the user agency of the experience. User agency in XR means to empower the user in their immersive digital journey. Crafting the level of interaction by using storytelling, while balancing curiosity and affordance, is the critical mission of UX designers conceptualizing immersive worlds in XR.

While this objective is clear in theory, we also need to look at the practical reality in typical use cases. What information do XR designers need to have, before committing to a platform, a toolset, or a framework, if they have a choice? During the very first initial ideation and discovery stage, where everything should be open and unrestricted, the focus is on the possible best solution for the user, without any thoughts on technical limitations or restrictions. Unrestricted user agency allows us to focus on the needs of the users, stepping into their shoes, doing research, and evaluating the needs and behaviors in the context of the larger goal, while in the next phase, when moving into design, which will ultimately lead to prototyping and testing, we need to commit to a toolset, platform, and framework, including its possibilities and limitations. Because of the wide variety of technologies, this step has severe implications in the way user agency and storytelling will play out and be perceived by the user.

This situation is dramatically different to traditional UX design, which has a much more streamlined process due to the limitations of UI interactions in web and mobile apps, the established conventions, mature tools, and the sophisticated ecosystem of prototyping and testing platforms.

In comparison, XR design is still the "Wild West" to some degree. A fact that will not change for some time, due to the much wider scope of technologies, tools, and platforms. One thing is for sure: XR designers have more hats to wear than UX designers for mobile and web applications. Next to fundamental understanding of the UX process and XR basics, knowledge of 3D and animation tools, a good understanding of the current state of solutions based on the Unity and Unreal engines, and a good understanding of the possibilities and limitations of the various frameworks, visual scripting solutions, and tools, plus the need to keep an eye on the ever-changing XR landscape. Frameworks are a way to organize and focus in this world of change and complexity.

3.4.1 The Importance of Frameworks for UX Design

Committing to a VR or AR framework means to accept its limitations, but also to take advantage of the presets and templates that have been provided to make prototyping faster and easier. But, even though it speeds up the process, frameworks still require the technical know-how of implementing their functions in the context of the unique design goals.

In the best-case scenario, a framework provides all the core components that are needed to get basic functionality set up, such as locomotion and basic object interaction, with the freedom to extend components and features, plus the ability to customize the look and feel of interactions and UI elements. In the best-case scenario, a framework can kick-start development with rapid prototyping that seamlessly transitions into the final product.

The analogy of an XR framework in the world of web development is, in a way, the open-source content management system WordPress. WordPress provides a framework structure plus a template and a plugin system that can be customized and fine-tuned with "What You See Is What You Get" (WYSIWYG) tools, which do not require coding.

WordPress was first released in 2003 and is an unparalleled success story, with now over a third of all Internet sites using it. As a user-friendly and powerful tool, WordPress is a showcase for how frameworks can take over the world, if they are open and flexible enough.

The WordPress story can in many ways be a role model for XR frameworks, where the technical complexities and dependencies are streamlined into framework solutions targeting specific use cases. The WordPress analogy also allows us to look at the importance of bespoke and original design-driven development, where no framework can match the design vision. In these cases, a custom design is handed over to the developer to be coded. While in the world of web and mobile apps, this handoff has a razor-sharp definition, typically executed in the typical waterfall process, this line is a lot blurrier in XR. The reason is that mature design and prototyping tools, such as Sketch, Figma, and Adobe XD, have developed a developer-friendly interface that makes the handoff crystal clear. There is practically no guesswork from the coding side when a UX/UI designer hands over a Figma-based prototype to be coded.

For original design-driven XR development that is not based on any framework, this interface does not exist at the current point in time. This in turn means that UX designers who are planning to create digital XR products based on custom designs need to resort to the toolset that UX designers were using before Sketch, XD, and Figma took center stage. These tools are as follows: the drawing board, mockups with Photoshop and After Effects, and any application that lets the designer communicate the design concept to a developer. The old-fashioned way of sketching and storyboarding is the core process of this approach. While this method may not be as fast as creating prototypes with a framework, it may in many cases be the preferred strategy, especially when the stakes are high, the budget is not restricted, and the project requires a commitment to a design vision that is not limited by framework constraints.

3.4.2 The Types of XR Projects and XR Designers

The decision to work with an XR framework is often driven by budget and time constraints. But it is also a question of other criteria, like: What type of project is it? What type of designer is executing the concept?

The reality is that the vast majority of XR projects are event-driven experiences for small and medium enterprises (SMEs), internal enterprise projects, or special programs involving organizations and institutions. The projects are typically for marketing events, trade show floors, experience areas in context of exhibitions, presentations and showcases, and custom-designed training situations. Typically, the projects are designed for a limited amount of headsets, where the final app is directly sideloaded on the individual headset. For VR projects, this process can be optimized by using the Oculus for Business solution that lets an organization manage a large fleet of headsets using cloud-based management tools. Most of these projects will never be listed on a public VR distribution network such as the Oculus store, Steam, or even the accessible SideQuest platform, because they are not public apps. Therefore, user testing has to be done in person with a handpicked representable group of users, unless the app is made available to remote users, via a downloadable app to sideload. These types of projects often have budget and time constraints, due to the limited circulation of these types of apps. The same limitations are often true for AR apps that are designed for special events, exhibitions, or museum programs. But, other than VR applications, typical handheld AR projects for special events don't need to supply the hardware, as users already own a smartphone or tablet; instead, the apps are distributed on the Apple and Google stores for download.

While the majority of VR projects are not in the public limelight, there is of course a lineup of VR applications that are publicly listed, because they have either been invited into the Oculus store or are distributed on

Steam or alternatively on the Oculus App Lab or SideQuest. The advantage is that user testing can have a wider reach and it is possible to build a community around a specific solution.

The different approaches, whether to use a framework and to be hands-on with prototyping, or the complete hands-off design-focused approach defines, in a way, the type of XR designer one strives to be.

Comparable to the definition of a full-stack developer in the software engineering field, one could define an XR designer who covers prototyping and final execution as a full-stack XR designer.

A full-stack XR designer, sometimes called a unicorn, would be able to conceptualize, design, prototype, and deliver the final XR application using available game engines, frameworks, and visual scripting tools or coding languages (Figure 3-7).

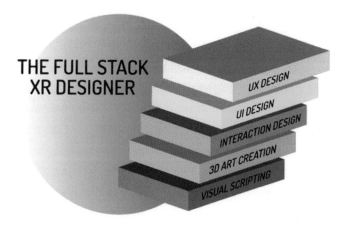

Figure 3-7. *The full-stack XR designer (image by C. Hillmann)*

Due to the wide responsibilities that fall under the UX design aspects of an XR designer, this would mean a lot of heavy lifting. Nevertheless, it is a powerful position to be in, as full control over look and feel, fine-tuning, visual detail, and interaction options falls directly under the hands of the designer. An XR designer who specializes in a specific framework can quickly prototype a solution and is flexible enough to tweak visual details, without any bottlenecks or guesswork. It allows the XR designer to take on small or large projects, without having to depend on a pipeline and external or internal team members, plus without having to worry about hand-off headaches. Another name for this type of XR designer is the XR Ninja, who knows everything, is aware of issues, knows how to work around problems, and uses all available tools to deliver professional results with fast turnaround times.

Is the full-stack XR designer/XR Ninja the superior professional compared to a traditional UX designer in the XR field? Not really. The traditional UX approach for digital XR products, where a clear line is drawn between design and coding, is very often preferred by clients, especially on larger enterprise projects. Under that definition, a designer conceptualizes; does research, ideation, and discovery; and then designs using traditional sketching and storytelling tools. Under this job definition, a design concept is handed over to the development team to build a prototype.

This model works best with larger teams and budgets and is often regarded as an ideal model, as every team member is an expert in their field with a dedicated core responsibility.

It should be noted that over the last two decades, the pressure on designers to do everything, including coding, has diminished. Instead, because of the overwhelming success of UX design in the digital economy, stakeholders often appreciate a specialist over a jack-of-all-trades. A UX designer in the XR space can be a specialist on just the design part, but the prerequisite of that role is, of course, profound knowledge of the technology and its possibilities, limitations, and dependencies.

3.5 XR Fundamentals: HCI, Usability, and UX

The study field of human-computer interaction (HCI) has entered an exciting era with the emerging technologies of immersive XR. The investigation of HCI research into how human senses, behaviors, and cognitive patterns interact with information technology was in many ways the forerunner of UX design and research. While XR designers typically deal with digital XR products that run on XR hardware, which has previously been designed through the design process of the hardware platform developer, it is nevertheless beneficial to investigate how the design of XR devices was conceived and conceptualized. Very often, it is a good idea to look at the design thinking behind a device to discover its design intentions.

3.5.1 VR Controllers and Usability Decisions

Author Blake J. Harris writes in his book *The History of the Future: Oculus, Facebook, and the Revolution That Swept Virtual Reality* about the internal discussions when the Oculus motion controllers were first developed. The controller team was on the mission to develop the ultimate universal controller that would give developers a maximum of freedom to create any possible VR experience. In this critical phase, fundamental decisions regarding the device's UX design had to be made. The decision on the path into the future was a result of fierce internal discussions. According to the book's records, the controller team, Palmer Luckey and Brendan Iribe, debated over the fundamental design philosophy and how a company like Apple, known for design-driven innovation, would approach a controller solution. The final result by Oculus ended up to be a compromise with traditional game controller functions, which set a standard for its intuitive design, functional flexibility, and superior comfort.

But it wasn't the only concept on the table. A puristic alternative could have been a minimalistic magic wand, in a way that Steve Jobs and Jony Ive would have envisioned it. During the internal discussions, this idea was dismissed, as a concept too much in line with the "form over function" philosophy of Apple. The Oculus management's decisions regarding the fundamental UX road map were most likely right, as the majority of its users were gamers. A totally different path would have been a simplified, minimalist magic wand as a single Oculus motion controller, which would have lowered the entry bar for new users and non-gamers, but would have severely limited the options for developers. Oculus stirred the device UX in the right direction. As it turns out, hand tracking without controllers, introduced a few years later, appears to be the path forward for casual users who are not comfortable using motion controllers.

3.5.2 The Form Follows Function Cliché in a UX Context

The "form follows function" vs. "form over function" debate in the context of VR hardware demonstrates how omnipresent this cliché still is, even though the quote is one of the most misunderstood statements in design history, despite being outdated and misinterpreted. An additional curiosity is the fact that the "form follows function" camp has been the adversary of UX thinking before its undisputed success and rise in the digital economy.

First of all, the quote is a layperson's design cliché that non-designers misattributed to classic modernist Bauhaus designers, while it was actually the American architect Louis Sullivan who stated it. Second, it is wrongly quoted; the original wording is "form ever follows function." The idea back then was that the design should reflect its purpose. The overuse of the misquoted and outdated phrase in popular culture then leads to the impression that function comes first and form, or design, comes second. This is in fact the direct opposite of what UX design is all about.

As a matter of fact, the layperson's "form follows function" doctrine and attitude was a burden to designers before the UX design boom through its unprecedented success. The general idea in the years before UX design took off, the decades before 2010, was this: Whenever new features are introduced through technical innovation, it is the role of design to make these features look appealing. This popular and widespread design misconception moved the designer to the end of the food chain. The designer was actually just there to make things look attractive, and the design work was more of an afterthought.

Numerous product train wrecks of the decades before 2010 are proof of this fatal approach: cluttered website menus, dashboards that were feature-rich but impossible to decipher, confusing pre-iOS smartphones, and hard-to-operate home entertainment gear. Designers were often forced to adapt their design ideas to a fixed feature lineup, with no information architecture, user research, and other essential UX concepts.

The UX revolution and its impact on the digital economy ended up turning things around and upside down. The designer was moved from the back seat to the front row, as the importance of UX design for the success of a digital product became indisputably apparent. Since the rise of UX, designers have been rightfully empowered to take the lead in the mission of developing successful products. Once the benefits became obvious, the UX design process was understood: Product features are of no or little value, if they don't contribute to the user's goals.

Nevertheless, the historical context of the "form follows function" era in the late nineteenth and early twentieth centuries is a fascinating period, where the conflict of technical feasibility and design decisions were fought out. The monuments of this struggle are still visible throughout the world. Skyscrapers influenced by the Bauhaus "form follows function" philosophy, but also by the opposite camp, represented by buildings like the Empire State Building in New York, where the architectural design was vision driven and not function driven.

This episode in architectural design is still fundamentally interesting, influential, and relevant concerning thoughts on design philosophy, and its impact still reverberates throughout other design fields.

It is striking to consider the interesting challenges that architectural designers had to face at that time: Technical innovation enabled architects to build higher office buildings with steel constructions. As the technical possibilities became clear, the question was: What would these new high-rise office buildings look like? Traditionally, high buildings were only national monuments and religious buildings such as church towers. The design thinking of that period was embedded in the belief that high buildings are monuments to the public eye and, therefore, should symbolize the spiritual aspiration of mankind. For that reason, many of the classic high rises embody ornamented steps that were borrowed from ancient temples. Bauhaus designers disrupted this line of thinking and presented the sober function-oriented philosophy. Today, we see examples of both camps as a reminder of that design struggle that turned Bauhaus into an international design movement. Both sides represent a rich and fascinating chapter of design history that reflects the recurring ideas of addressing technical innovation with design decisions.

3.5.3 What UX Really Means for XR

The rapid technological innovation in the XR space forces designers to adapt and often find solutions that have been proven in comparable situations, where a paradigm shift required unconventional ideas and out-of-the-box thinking about the fundamentals of human-machine interaction. An often quoted example is the invention of the computer mouse by Douglas Engelbart in 1964. The problem was obvious in hindsight: how to interact with a computer screen in a fast, efficient, and comfortable way. Fast forward to 2020 and we see a similar question still unanswered regarding AR interaction: Are gestures and hand tracking really the best solution for AR headset? Or is there a design solution that could offer an even better experience to the user, addressing the issues of hand fatigue and lack of haptic feedback? One innovative company in this niche is Litho.cc, which makes the intriguing suggestive statement: "The mouse was for the computer. The...is for Augmented Reality." The small and clever Litho controller is an innovative solution to address the shortcomings of hand input or traditional controllers. We will most likely see more of these highly focused and UX-driven input devices that are targeting the pain points of XR interaction (Figure 3-8).

Figure 3-8. *The input evolution (from left to right): mouse, game controller, motion controller, hand tracking, Litho controller (image by C. Hillmann)*

For UX designers developing digital XR products, that means this: not only more opportunities but also more responsibilities and more things to learn and test. While the hardware UX is provided by the device developer, the UX design for digital experiences built on the platform has to take advantage of the technology, but also guide the user through the features that are device dependent. From the user's perspective, there is often no difference between hardware and software UX, as it is perceived as a single entity most of the time. With that in mind, XR designers have the opportunity to deliver exceptional experiences, especially when a deeper understanding of platform technology and device options helps in the design process.

3.6 Summary

This chapter looked at the role of the UX designer in the digital economy and how the changes in the game industry influenced the definition of game design and ultimately UX design. It evaluated emerging VR standards and how XR frameworks became increasingly important for UX design decisions. The chapter looked at typical project categories and how timeless design philosophies and fundamental questions of device UX connect with digital XR products in the UX process.

CHAPTER 4

UX and Experience Design: From Screen to 3D Space

4.1 Introduction

This chapter will break down the UX elements that define the spatial nature of XR. It will look at the evolution of the 3D design space, its unique characteristics and features, to review the potential UX challenges by empathizing with the user. The chapter will narrow down a strategy to apply UX design techniques to a digital XR product, taking into account the 3D object characteristics of its components as well as considering the importance of mindful design for its long-term success.

The spatial nature of AR and VR experiences makes 3D navigation and 3D content a native core ingredient in the user interaction. The VR world is experienced with stereoscopic depth; AR glasses enable the discovery of digital overlays that are embedded into the user's depth perception of the environment. Even handheld AR applications for smartphones and tablets, which are displayed on a flat screen, interact with the 3D world through spatial movement and 3D navigation. The real world is a 3D space, where objects are measured on the X, Y, and Z axes. A flat-panel display (FPD)

© Cornel Hillmann 2021
C. Hillmann, *UX for XR*, https://doi.org/10.1007/978-1-4842-7020-2_4

device, on the other hand, a monitor or tablet screen, flattens and simplifies the 3D world, which in turn makes the content often easier to process. The third dimension, contrarily, unlocks new superpowers for the user, by taking advantage of the additional layers an information architecture in an immersive and stereoscopic XR interaction space can provide.

4.2 Creative Solutions for the XR Friction Funnel

As the XR revolution is moving the user interaction from the flat screen into an immersive 3D space, it is of utmost importance to not lose the user or the qualities that made user interaction so successful for digital products in the mobile era.

Over its history, technology has continuously provided humans with superpowers, and society had to take its time to adapt to them. Driven by attractive promises such as "be as fast as a horse" (motorized vehicle) and "talk to people far away" (phone), the human brain needed to learn and understand these new superpowers as part of its upgraded toolset. Evolution has taught our species to be able to quickly adapt to new opportunities, especially if they provided a shortcut, made things easier and faster, but were still rooted in our deeper assumptions about the nature of reality.

The UX design process has been exceptionally successful for the wave of innovation on mobile and web platforms, while design innovation on these platforms is still pushing forward with moderate speed and every year's design trend breathes fresh air into design cycles and feature iterations. It is now a level playing field where users, designers, and stakeholders understand which features drive retention and what the user expects from the interaction with a design. Every swipe, touch interaction, and gesture has been carefully mapped and measured, while newer interaction methods, such as voice user interface (VUI), are carefully introduced, following UX design principles and research.

Comparing the well-refined standards and the organic growth of the mobile and web space to the experimental XR field makes the latter look somewhat like the Wild West in comparison.

Part of this struggle is because a 3D XR space has a number of inherent pitfalls and potential problems, due to the higher complexity and the increased number of ways a user can interact with a design, when it is distributed along three instead of two axes.

To find out what the important considerations are that make or break a successful user experience in a digital 3D space, it makes sense to look at the problem from a fundamental perspective, that is, looking at the evolution of interaction and UX/UI design and what takeaways can bring value into the problem-solving process.

Another consideration is, what problems does a 3D space solve for a user interacting with it? How are the 3D superpowers of an immersive digital space benefitting the user?

4.2.1 The UI Evolution into 3D Space

If we look back at the last 20 years of UX/UI design, it becomes obvious that UX/UI designers and 3D interaction had very few touchpoints (with the sole exception of game UI design, which developed independently). As a matter of fact, one of the biggest UX/UI design innovations that paved the way for today's UI standards was the rise of flat design, which is quite the opposite of a 3D visualization.

Flat design's minimalistic approach made user interaction easier, clearer, and more focused. It is performance-friendly and highly adaptive for responsive designs; plus it looked pixel-perfect sharp and made visual harmony easier to design, by using a flat color palette. The result was increased usability and a style that developed into its own art movement.

Looking at pre-flat design interfaces from today's design perspective gives the impression of a hopelessly outdated paradigm. Beveled buttons and 3D elements representing real-world elements, called skeuomorphism, often added confusion instead of clarity.

Flat design cleaned up the clutter in interface design that had spread throughout the previous decades, and it created a new usability standard for the mobile era.

Apple's original Skeuomorphism evolved into Microsoft's Fluent and Google's Material Design, emphasizing efficiency instead of familiarity of a design language using 3D aesthetics.

Nevertheless, it didn't take too long until subtle 3D elements were carefully reintroduced into the flat paradigm. Minor 3D accents, such as soft shadows and carefully stacked UI panels with ambient occlusion, found their way into modern interface design to help navigate the information architecture, when it was necessary to emphasize the layer order using hints toward a third dimension. When 3D was reintroduced back into interface design, it was evaluated through the UX design process. This time around, with a focus on usability and user benefits, instead of visual gimmicks using 3D techniques, just because they were available. Mimicking depth with shadows and highlights was a way to address some of the areas of critique that flat design had to face, mainly problems of determining the function of designs and distinguishing UI navigation elements. The data-driven move away from some of the purist flat design principles enabled a new wave of design innovation, including a skeuomorphic renaissance, with branches such as neumorphism and glassmorphism.

3D in visual interface design is a very specific area, while interactive 3D in the larger context of the UX design process is really a different game altogether, but the interaction use cases and design approaches of how to communicate and interact with spatial elements in a 3D layout are an interesting case study, considering it's evolution in design history.

The takeaway for XR design is this: It is a good idea to take the minimum viable product (MVP) approach and focus on the features and design elements that are most important to the users, by asking questions such as "What is the minimum feature set and design solution to solve a given problem?", and "How can I reduce the core function to a minimum to be able to test if it is moving in the right direction and is working for the user?" This approach, often called the Lean UX Loop, is an iterative process of observing, building, testing, and measuring. The general MVP methodology is universal and applies to interaction design as much as visual design (Figure 4-1).

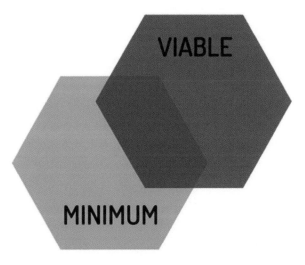

Figure 4-1. *The minimum viable product. A minimum product is a less attractive product because it has fewer features. A viable product has all the features it could have, but is too expensive. The minimum viable product is an intersection of both and typically good for start-ups to test the validity of a product for a given market (image by C. Hillmann)*

4.2.2 Understanding the User in the Funnel

John Carmack, developer legend, previous CTO, and currently consulting CTO of Oculus, often talked about the friction funnel problem of VR, that is, the amount of time and the effort a person has to undertake to finally get to the desired immersive experience. A lot of the factors that play into the friction funnel are determined by the hardware, and UX designers for digital products can't do much about it, besides hoping that the next-generation headset will be lighter, faster, and easier to wear.

Nevertheless, UX designers have control over the digital product experience and especially the onboarding process, the first impression, and the crucial first 30–60 seconds of an experience. A good design can help to guide the user in a stimulating and informative way, to jump-start the XR journey with the positive initial impact of a helpful and entertaining onboarding process.

Due to its immersive nature, the first impression in XR is much more intense and therefore much more important for a positive user experience. No other electronic medium carries as much risk, when the loading screen takes too long; the first images stutter, lag, or are distorted; or the initial landing space suffers from disorientation and lack of guidance. The fact that a VR user often launches from an empty dark space makes it often very disruptive for the casual user.

Developers repeatedly underestimate the worries of users: Is this going to be tedious, boring, troublesome, and annoying? The time it takes to lift the user out of an endless black space often seems to last an eternity, if no positive stimulus is given. Not as drastic, but in some ways similar, is the loading time starting up an AR application. Very often, users worry about missing something or looking the wrong way or are nervous that there may be something they will not comprehend. Developers therefore need UX designers for exactly that reason: user empathy.

User empathy is the cornerstone of every successful digital product design. Understanding the user and using techniques such as empathy mapping is typically an essential step in the problem-solving process (Figure 4-2).

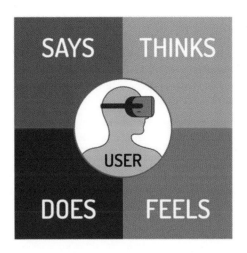

Figure 4-2. *Empathy mapping is linked to the used product. The case study in Chapter 6 is an example of how empathy mapping and sensual input play out in XR (image by C. Hillmann)*

An empathy map is based on user research, interviews, and surveys with the goal to articulate the needs of a particular type of user or user segment. The empathy map can be used as a base to extract personas, during the early stages of the UX design process. The four quadrants "Says, Thinks, Does, and Feels" are assessed to capture the user's behavior and attitude. "Says" can be direct quotes from research, while "Thinks" defines what is important to the user. "Does" is the action a user takes to reach their goal, and "Feels" refers to the emotional attitude, the worries and excitement of the experience. This map then allows us to draw conclusions during the first stages of the design process to find a user-centered solution. It is one of many tools to understand user behavior, identify the pain points, remove bias, and communicate the findings within a team.

Next to this process, there are a number of established recipes in immersive media design, to manage the onboarding stage:

– First of all: Do it step by step and introduce new things in small increments.

– Second: Show something familiar that makes people feel comfortable.

– Third: Give a taste of the world that the user is entering, a tiny preview of the style, scale, design concept, mood, and vision.

– And fourth: Do something joyful or interesting at the very beginning, to induce a positive attitude.

Very often, XR experiences use the initial height assessment, or controller setup, to make a good first impression using gamified content. If the user receives affirmation that things were done in the right way, they may feel much more positive and willing to commit.

Well-designed VR experiences put a lot of emphasis on fast loading, a good-looking loading screen with unique audio branding followed by an attractive lobby equipped with interactive objects to explore.

In a similar way, well-balanced AR applications bring on early eye candy, put high emphasis on spatial audio design, and give early orientation hints in a way that makes entering the interaction feel organic and natural.

4.2.3 The XR World Is 3D, Just Like the Real World

As pointed out in the beginning of this chapter, the elements of XR design live in a 3D space. Even a flat single four-sided polygon is a spatial object in that sense, because in relationship to the user, it can change its relative position through the distance and viewing angle. For example, some prototyping tools allow the export of photoshop layers with a spatial offset on the Z axis to be important as an AR object. In this way, a previously flat design becomes a 3D object with added 3D dimensions. This fact raises a host of new questions for the designer. For example:

> How can I avoid perspective distortion, as a result of the viewing angle?

> What is the optimal distance to the viewer, and how can I make sure the best distance is accomplished and maintained?

> How does my design interact with the environment? Does it reflect colors and light? Where does it cast shadows? Is it part of the environment? Does it sit on a surface or does it float?

The questions don't stop with just the appearance; object interaction also brings on a whole new round of questions, such as:

> Does the object react to approximation? How is it activated? What visual feedback will be given when it is activated? Will it rotate, light up, or grow in size, or will it be outlined with a glow?

Some of these questions can be addressed with traditional game design solutions: Camera-facing planes can be accomplished by using the classic game billboard, forcing objects to always face the camera or the user's perspective. In a similar way, floating menus that follow the user's movement can help to stabilize the optimal viewing angle and viewing distance. As mentioned in the previous chapter, a lot of experimentation that went into VR UI solutions can be applied to AR. On the other hand, interaction frameworks that have been established for AR, such as the MRTK (Mixed Reality Toolkit) framework prioritizing hand interaction, may also find their way into VR, where they are applicable.

4.2.4 3D Navigation as a Superpower

A 3D interaction space has an enormous potential to benefit the user, but also an additional amount of pitfalls where it can fail.

The benefit of an immersive and stereoscopic UX is that we get an additional depth axis for interaction and a 360-degree space to organize information. The goal is to have faster access to the content, to easily understand the context of it, and to have more room to spread it out. If we look at the evolution of UX/UI design, it becomes obvious that one of the recurring challenges has been the organization of the information architecture through a user interface, as often reflected in complex menus and submenus.

An immersive 3D space that can be experienced with stereoscopic depth perception, on the other hand, opens up new opportunities to organize and present complex information, using depth perception and immersive space superpowers.

In the XR world, we can actually reach behind an object, move an item from front to back, or swivel an information container into position, without causing confusion as it would on a 2D screen.

Once again, the MRTK framework is a good showcase, for how this can be done in an elegant and intuitive way.

The most effective interaction design follows patterns that the human brain already understands and knows. Hand or controller gestures to press, unfold, switch, flip, roll up, and turn over digital elements work well in XR because we are familiar with them from our real-world experience and have an expectation of the outcome. There is an additional element of satisfaction, when seeing something that works in real life being reproduced in AR or VR. It gives a user the comforting idea that interaction principles are universal and that their knowledge and experience is valid in any possible place, real or virtual.

Next to reinforcing the familiar, the exaggeration and enhanced XR abilities enable a sense of empowerment in the user. Being able to pull things from a distance with gravity pull, moving with fast teleportation, and other enhanced interaction methods introduce superpowers that are based on familiar ideas and serve as shortcuts to get to results faster. XR superpowers need to have a strong reason, like a major user benefit, to exist, and they need to be communicated to the user, who might otherwise not know about them. The onboarding process is a good opportunity to introduce the user to the basic concepts and give an early taste of the benefits. Focusing on a well-paced gamified feature introduction has often been a winning formula for successful titles while at the same time minimizing the user's friction funnel entering an XR experience.

4.3 The Fundamentals of Designing Spatial XR Experiences

We are entering an era where the lines will be increasingly blurred between physical and digital experiences. Consequently, designers are encouraged to understand the role of spatial design in the physical world as much as its rules in the digital world. The sensory and atmospheric qualities of a space and how to translate the spatial design language into the XR world are a good starting point. Experiences from architects, interior designers, and stage designers help us to understand how to design a spatial journey and how to map positive and negative space, active or inactive space. Spatial memory, visibility, depth, and the psychology of shared spaces are important considerations in the spatial design process. The role of space in design has a rich cultural history and can be reflected in both micro spaces down to UI elements and macro spaces, such as the experience area and entire XR world and its storytelling. World building and spatial design are the key ingredients, next to interaction design and digital object design, to build convincing and meaningful digital places.

4.3.1 The UX Design Process for Digital XR Products

UX principles are universal and apply to anything, be it digital or real-world interaction with any object design, down to common everyday items such as a simple teacup. The same goes for the general UX design process in its essential phases: product definition, research, analysis, design, and validation. This process is universal and true for any design category, may it be digital or not. When zooming in on the UX design process for web and mobile apps vs. XR experiences, the difference lies in the efficiency of the iterative process (Figure 4-3).

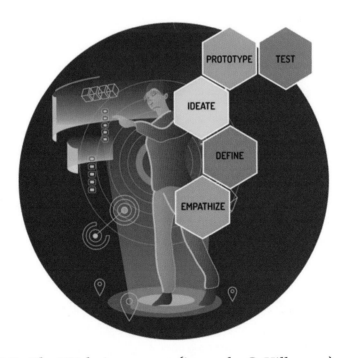

Figure 4-3. *The UX design process (image by C. Hillmann)*

While the general UX design process is universal, it is the efficiency of the iterative process that has given rise to the enormous success stories of the mobile era. The highly efficient pipeline from low-fidelity to high-fidelity prototype and the established protocols for the developer handoff have powered the agile product design revolution with a highly dynamic energy. To transfer this undisputed winning formula to digital XR products, we need to look at the pain points in the XR prototyping process. These are, as previously pointed out, a much higher platform complexity, a much higher count of interaction types, and often a lack of interaction standards. This in turn means that building a prototype to test and iterate is a much more demanding endeavor, requiring either a high level of technical skills or the support of a coding team. Building, testing, and iterating is very straightforward for web and mobile applications, because there is a limited set of interaction types between click, touch, and swipe. UX design tools for web and mobile apps, like Sketch, Figma, and Adobe XD, have narrowed down the most important functions, interaction types, and transitions, to be able to build a clickable prototype on the fly. This rapid design process enhanced by powerful tools, transitioning from low-fidelity to high-fidelity prototype, to quickly test and iterate, has given UX design the important edge and turned it into a booming industry.

To be able to strive toward a similar level of efficiency using the UX design process for digital XR products, however, we need to identify and map the areas containing potential bottlenecks.

4.3.2 The Double Diamond in XR

The famous double diamond is probably one of the most fundamental standards for UX design. It shows the two stages of research and design and conveys the divergent vs. convergent thinking in the UX design process through its distinct diamond shape. The first diamond shows the process of finding the problem: discovering it (divergent) followed by defining it (convergent). The second diamond goes through the process of finding a solution: ideation, spreading out connections (divergent), followed by narrowing down results, implementing and testing them (convergent) (Figure 4-4).

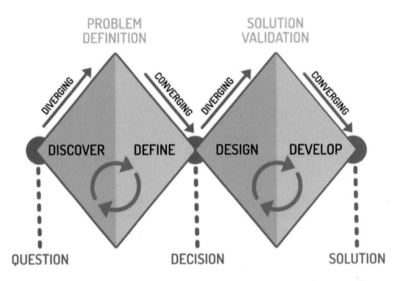

Figure 4-4. *The double diamond and XR mapping (image by C. Hillmann)*

It can be argued that the most critical point for XR is in between the two diamonds—the space after defining the problem and before the solution-finding process. This spot in the middle is classically defined as the final brief, which is a synthesis of the research phase, that frames the actual design process. Here's one way to look at it: From this point onward, we need to consider the conditions of the XR world, to be able to, later, successfully prototype and iterate. If we don't consider the condition of the XR world at this critical point, especially in terms of efficiency, we may run into major problems later in the process, for example, the ideation process during the second diamond resulting in a dead end, because the results are impossible to implement or too time consuming and difficult to prototype. One approach is to capture the conditions and the nature, plus the platform constraints of the XR environment at this stage. From the many possible ways to address this stage, there is one particular system that is an excellent candidate to fill the gap: Object-Oriented UX (OOUX).

4.3.3 UX Design Innovation: OOUX

What is OOUX? Designing a digital product for spatial computing, to be used on contemporary AR or VR devices, means to conceptualize solutions for a 3D space. Every XR object, even simple 2D overlays, lives in a 3D context and is experienced with spatial dependencies. To approach specific design problems, we can look at the design strategy, either from a task-oriented or, alternatively, from an object-oriented perspective. While the traditional way is task focused, using storytelling and use cases to solve problems, it makes sense to approach spatial computing with an object-oriented design method, to capture the nature of the spatial XR world that is populated with digital 3D objects.

Object-Oriented UX (OOUX) is a design philosophy that focuses on objects, that is, the things users interact with. OOUX is inspired by object-oriented programming (OOP), which is a software design paradigm focused on data objects over functions and logic.

OOUX evangelist Sophia V. Prater (objectorientedux.com) pointed out in an conversation about XR:

> "If we are designing a digital environment—through the medium of screens, or voice UI, or virtual reality—we designers need to get intimately clear on what objects need to be in that environment. What objects will be valuable to the end user? How do these objects relate to each other? What can users do to these objects? And what attributes might these objects have? If we don't get clear on these fundamental questions before implementing

our designs, it's unlikely that we will make the
answers readily clear to our users. If users can't
easily understand the objects in an environment,
there is little chance that they will understand the
environment itself."

The object-oriented approach organizes the UX design process by
classifying objects first and then assigning actions to these objects. The
benefit is that it follows the mindset of the user who first looks at an object
and then decides what to do with it. The user journey and its objects
and calls for action are a reflection of how people behave in real life. For
example, when entering a building, a person is looking for things, objects,
to interact with, for example, an elevator, followed by the elevator button to
activate it.

While OOUX is a distinct methodology to solving UX design problems
on any platform, its general approach is a good match for the design
problems in the XR world. The reasons are as follows:

1. OOUX is more efficient to address the XR space. As
   spatial computing is naturally object oriented, the
   mental models of OOUX are often identical to the
   actual XR objects.

2. OOUX addresses the core content as objects before
   considering procedural actions. The responsive
   nature of OOUX makes it platform independent and
   its philosophy and flexibility free from paradigms
   geared toward pages and UX/UI processes tied to
   the web and mobile space on 2D screens.

3. XR prototyping is often OOP based (like Blueprints
   in the Unreal Engine 4). It is easier and more
   consistent to stay within an object-oriented mindset.

In my book *Unreal for Mobile and Standalone VR* (Apress 2019, ISBN 978-1-4842-4360-2), I talk about how important it is for noncoders to get into the object-oriented mindset when designing VR worlds using OOP-based visual scripting. Chapter 3, "The Object-Oriented Mindset: Converting Ideas into Blueprints," pages 66–69, explains the benefits of having functions encapsulated in objects and the importance of object inheritance, as a fundamental way of object-oriented thinking, to be more efficient with VR production using the Unreal engine and its Blueprint system.

Object-oriented thinking is an obvious choice with programming-related problems, but also scales well beyond that. It is no surprise that the OOP revolution has been a major influence in other areas, such as on design and philosophy. As a matter of fact, the class-based object-oriented programming paradigm has been foreshadowed in ancient ideas, such as Plato's *theory of form*. Plato describes forms as abstract representations of the real-world objects, which correlates very closely to the modern OOP mindset.

The big ideas behind OOUX not only help to structure, align, and prioritize a digital system; they also help to solve problems up to the granular level while always staying aligned to a user's expectations of the physical world.

OOUX removes the clutter and structures the core content into an XR-friendly information architecture. It offers an excellent solution for the XR-mapping process between the "problem definition" diamond and the "solution validation" diamond in the UX double diamond process.

OOUX creator and evangelist Sophia Prater of objectorientedux. com uses a specific methodology called the ORCA process to break down objects, relationships, calls to actions, and attributes, in the transition from research to design at the center of the UX double diamond process. ORCA stands for Object discovery, Relationship discovery, Call-to-Action discovery, and Attribute discovery.

4.3.4 OOUX in Action

The goal of OOUX is to think of content first and identify reusable, interchangeable, modular things: a modular system that reflects real-world mental models to be applied to any platform or device with efficiency and consistency. Within the typical UX design process, the OOUX steps are as follows:

1. Discover objects.

    Using research data, such as stakeholder and user interviews, the objects can be directly extracted from the goals of an organization or a user story, by finding the nouns associated with it.

2. Define objects.

    The core content that defines an object are the granular descriptions that make it up. Defining purpose, attributes, and metadata also establishes a shared language over what defines the object.

3. Establish object relationships.

    Object relationships are established by cross-referencing or nesting using thought experiments on each object and its relationships to others.

4. Force rank objects.

    Prioritizing and ranking objects means reducing complexity to what is most important. The focus is on core features that could be used for an MVP.

Typically done on a whiteboard with colored sticky notes, this process creates clarity with a content structure that is modular, responsive, and reusable.

OOUX is most often used for web and mobile design, where it quickly translates into low-fidelity wireframes to be able to iterate quickly from there. Due to its high level of abstraction, it can convert to any device or platform, including the XR space.

The advantage in the XR space is that OOUX objects naturally translate into a XR prototype referencing actual digital objects and their functions.

4.3.5 Case Study: Reality UX

Having mapped out an object-oriented design system is the foundation to the next stage: to build a prototype. How to go about it depends on a number of factors, including technical skills of the designers and technical team availability, plus framework and platform limitations.

I have come up with an in-house system that I will use as a case study. The idea behind it is to address the typical problems of the prototyping stage in XR. The solution is called Reality UX (rUX), which is an umbrella term for the process to solve UX XR problems using OOUX, XR heuristics, and our in-house solution called the Reality UX toolkit (Figure 4-5).

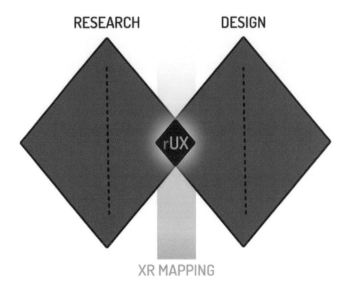

RESEARCH   **DESIGN**

rUX

XR MAPPING

Figure 4-5. *The double diamond and XR mapping with Reality UX (rUX) (image by C. Hillmann)*

What is the Reality UX toolkit? The Reality UX toolkit contains everything needed to design a low-fidelity prototype that seamlessly scales to high-fidelity prototype for testing and iteration. At its center, it has an inventory of the features in the most common XR frameworks, such as the Unity XR interaction toolkit, the Mixed Reality Toolkit (MRTK), and the Advanced VR Framework for the Unreal Engine 4, among others. Using a unique identifier, each feature is referenced with a letter followed by a number, plus a description of the function, for example, "A04— teleportation using the UE4 Advanced VR Framework," followed by description and feature set. As each framework has its unique functions, interaction solutions, and customization options, the Reality UX toolbox keeps track of all available options in a database. The Reality UX database is updated when needed, for example, when new versions, or completely new framework additions, become available.

The system serves as a reference library, to easily identify specific framework functions on a specific platform. The goal is to eliminate the guesswork, when moving from ideation to low-fidelity prototype to MVP.

It addresses the problem that very often, at the sketching and ideation stage, functions are unclear and consequently difficult to prototype. For example, a function in an XR concept would require custom coding, creating a bottleneck that would have been easy to avoid if identified earlier as a generic framework solution that does the same thing and is available out of the box. The benefit of locking functions to specific framework features at the ideation stage is that it creates a much clearer road map to implementation while still having enough flexibility to point out custom features (with their own unique identifier, such C001 and so on), to be considered from early on.

Using the Reality UX toolkit, a UX designer can identify framework functions while sketching them with pen and paper, using simple identifiers that team members can look up, review, and test, before building a design, if needed.

This solution has enough flexibility for different approaches and use cases. For example, in a completely open ideation process, where any platform and function is completely open, a mix-and-match approach can be used to mix different framework identifiers and custom functions together while later in the process narrowing it down to the most important ones that make it easier to finally decide which platform and framework to choose. It helps to identify early where a framework can deliver a solution and where a required function requires custom coding or scripting.

Or, in a completely different approach, limit the selection to one specific framework and platform to move faster into the prototyping process.

The idea behind the Reality UX toolkit is to mimic the clarity of the UX design process for web and mobile apps, when designing clickable prototypes, and to build on clearly defined features and functions, for example, a button click triggers a page transition. A low-fidelity prototype is able to reference the functions of a high-fidelity prototype and final product, because the functions are so clearly defined.

The Reality UX toolkit as a database is a living document, where features, comments, problems, and customization options are tracked and updated in a shared format that is accessible to team members.

Identifying functions of available frameworks at an early design stage is a way to avoid headaches and bottlenecks later on, when a solution that looks easy on paper turns out to be an unnecessary technical challenge. Frameworks are almost always equipped with the standard base interactions that don't need to be reinvented unless there is a specific reason to do so.

The general XR problem-solving approach depends on the type of project and especially the budget and team size. Some projects may require custom coding from start to finish, because specific cutting-edge multiplayer performance or other innovative features are required.

The Reality UX example is one of many possible ways to address the prototyping process in XR, which is especially useful not only for mid-size projects but also smaller applications, including one-offs, for example, special event experiences and enterprise sandboxes for in-house use. Its advantage is this: fast and reliable results using proven methods and established framework functions to bring a project from ideation to MVP in as little time as possible.

Considering the context of OOUX, the process to get there is as follows:

1. Using OOUX to identify the mental objects and information architecture

2. Designing a concept by assigning visual objects to the mental models from OOUX

3. Identifying functions and referencing them using the Reality UX toolbox

4. Building and iterating using the referenced framework functions

4.3.6 3D, Spatial Object Design and User Interaction

After having discussed the UX design process for digital XR products and its specific problems, it is a good idea to look at 3D object design and what role it plays in spatial computing. 3D objects have different roles and definitions in AR and VR.

In VR, the virtual space is populated with 3D objects that make up the environment and create the illusion of space and depth. Each VR world is a unique 3D object architecture. 3D objects are game engine assets and form the building blocks of an immersive VR design.

The majority of 3D objects in AR, which is currently dominated by handheld AR, follow a different set of rules, at least at the present stage of the industry.

AR objects most often don't live in their own distinct worlds, but rather on platforms, and the AR interaction is most often enabled by social media applications, such as Snapchat and Facebook, or by dedicated AR-sharing platforms, such as Adobe Aero. 3D objects for handheld AR are very often self-contained applications instead of being part of an immersive environment. This situation could quickly change, in case specific AR applications become popular enough to change the overall dynamic of the industry, as it happened with *Pokemon Go* or with the IKEA AR app *IKEA Place* and related success stories, mostly in the "product tryout" category. Still, the majority of social AR interactions take place through social and sharing platforms and are focused on individual AR objects. Its role can be interpreted as follows: The AR object is the app.

A typical example is the way Apple promotes special events by sending a link with an invitation. The link opens an AR object, utilizing Apple's AR platform features such as AR Quick Look, to reveal an AR object embedded in the user's environment. After activation, the AR object plays an animation and releases its information.

The benefit of AR objects is such that the user feels a sense of ownership, because the object is revealed in their very own immediate environment. It is part of their world, and it reacts according to their actions and environment changes. This fact makes the object more intimate and personal, and it is easier to establish a personal relationship with the user that encourages interaction.

The concept, that is, the AR object is the app, has a number of implications for UX designers. At the center of the visual design of an AR object is the 3D polygonal design, texture design, and 3D animation, wrapped up in a spatial storytelling concept.

UX/UI designers moving into spatial storytelling will have to transition from 2D to 3D design to build the visual components and the interactions that enable and drive the XR narrative.

4.3.7 The Social AR Object As an App and How to Design It

The visual design process of an AR asset is similar to that of a 3D game or VR asset, with the difference that AR objects often stand on their own if designed for a sharing platform. The visual design attributes that define its appeal are dependent on the platform's features and the user's environment.

To design a shareable social AR app or object, it is important to verify the supported feature set by addressing the following questions: Does it support multiple animations? What trigger options are available? What kinds of information can be revealed? What shading options and environment features are available?

Central to the AR object is its visual appeal. A user will only be interested to engage and interact, if the presented object looks interesting and appealing enough. One of the big unique selling points of AR objects is the fact that they embed into the user's environment, which is typically accomplished with the camera's see-through function and object tracking on handheld devices, through Apple's ARKit and Google's ARCore technology.

The key features that are required to embed an AR object convincingly into the user's environment are surface shadows and object environment shading. Surface shadows are handled by the platform, and there is very little a designer can do to tweak the quality of how the shadow from an AR object is projected on the user's environment surface. Object AR surfaces, on the other hand, are under the designer's control. How an object interacts with the environment light is determined by the design of its surface shaders.

The computer graphic standard for photorealistic real-time shading is called Physically Based Rendering (PBR), a concept that splits the surface characteristics into dedicated channels, using textures maps to define surface properties. PBR texturing has been a staple and important craft in game asset design. Most modern games depend heavily on detailed PBR textures to convey realism and environment details. Tools such as Adobe Substance Painter and Marmoset Toolbag offer a rich toolset to design surface materials, by painting or tweaking the respective channel texture maps. The most common and basic PBR channels are the Albedo (color) map, the normal map, the roughness map, the metalness map, and the ambient occlusion map.

This set of the five base channels is often enough for common surface properties in a majority of objects (Figure 4-6).

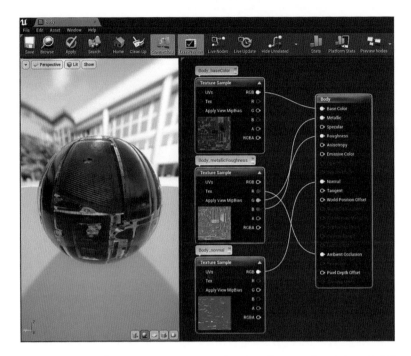

Figure 4-6. *Unreal Engine 4 material PBR channels, using RGB channel packing for ambient occlusion, metalness, and roughness*

Using and designing these channels will determine how the environment light is picked up from the device's camera and how it interacts with the AR object that uses PBR textures.

AR objects are only convincing if they convey the discrete visual cues—ambient lighting, reflection, self-shadowing, and specular highlights—from an environment. Each PBR material channel contributes to the realistic surface interaction with the light source, which, most of the time, is based on High-Dynamic-Rage (HDR) image lighting, synthesized by the camera in real time.

PBR texturing for an AR object is an important part of its appeal, but it also depends on general style decisions. Some designers may prefer minimal, limited, or simple textureless non-PBR shading for stylized context or in cases where the download size needs to be kept at a minimum.

The other important part of an appealing AR object are its animations. The animation brings the object to life and communicates its state and its message or call to action. Very often, AR objects have an idle state animation loop that signals "waiting for activation" and a trigger-activated, play-once animation that reveals the information or mission, often a call to action, web link, or announcement.

The features of sharable AR objects are constrained to the feature set of each AR social media authoring platform, like Spark AR Studio for Facebook and Instagram and Lens Studio for Snapchat. Other AR object sharing platforms, like Adobe Aero, require an AR viewing app to be installed on the device. Next to the platform authoring constraints is the 3D object format that defines the visual design process.

The following are the contemporary 3D object file formats used in AR:

1. glTF (Graphics Language Transmission Format) by the Khronos Group, an open industry consortium

2. USDZ (Universal Scene Description, zip-compressed), created by Apple in partnership with Pixar

Both formats have similar features, are fast, and support PBR textures as well as animations.

These modern file formats replace the established FBX exchange format that has been a standard for VFX and game development and the legacy OBJ format (for only geometry and UV data, without textures and animations).

A basic USDZ or glTF object can store all the necessary visual information, such as PBR materials and object animations, and it is viewable in AR through Apple's iOS Quick Look AR viewer or any AR model viewer on Android devices. An excellent showcase of XR models is the platform Sketchfab.com, which allows the review of 3D models with PBR textures and animations in both AR and VR, including a way to review the individual PBR channels and wireframe through its model inspector. Sketchfab is not only a premier marketplace for XR assets but also a great learning resource that allows aspiring XR designers to study the construction of premium production assets, by analyzing the components that bring it to life (Figure 4-7).

Figure 4-7. *The model inspector in Sketchfab, with a model by Nika Tendetnik (CC BY 4.0, sketchfab.com/n.tendetnik)*

The visual design of AR assets and their geometry, surface attribute, and animation, plus the interaction features of the AR authoring platform, are the critical ingredients to author convincing AR objects that can be shared via social media and dedicated AR channels.

The techniques are to a great degree identical for VR, regarding model and surface properties, but due to the fact that VR assets are typically part of a larger closed environment authored by a game engine, VR-specific techniques and conventions have to be considered (as pointed out in Chapter 3).

The social AR object as an app is currently the most popular AR concept, due to the wide use of AR-handled devices and the popular use of AR features on social media platforms. That may change in the near future as wearable AR devices become more accessible and dedicated AR experiences, with richly populated immersive and stereoscopic AR environments, may rise to mainstream popularity.

4.4 Immersive Interaction: Senses, Haptics, Gestures, Audio, and Voice

The user experience in XR is the result of the sum of its sensual inputs. We can design how the human brain processes this input, by crafting a user journey using sight, hearing, and touch. Occasionally, we come across an extended toolbox for the senses, when experimental experiences are using smell, taste, and thought. Through controlled user interaction, using the brain-computer interface (BCI) is still highly experimental, but it will make it to consumer devices in a few years' time.

Sight, hearing, and touch are the fundamental components of a contemporary XR experience, using immersive visual design, spatial audio, and haptic controller feedback. Giving visual, audio, and touch stimuli allows us to direct the user's attention and send them on the storytelling journey, revealing content, activating and unlocking relevant building blocks that make this experience satisfying, worthwhile, and meaningful.

The immersive nature of XR means visual and audio cues can come from anywhere in a 360 environment. Being able to visually sense stereoscopic depth and identify the exact location of a spatial audio cue offers opportunities to engage the user in ways not possible on other media platforms.

360 3D environments and spatial audio have been part of game design for 2D monitors since the rise of computer gaming into the mainstream, but the new ingredient that now changes everything is the fact that the

environment for XR wearables is stereoscopic and immersive, with the user at its center, interacting with a real-life simulation. A sound from behind can trigger the instinct to turn around, and visual cues, such as object highlights while raycasting, can signal affordance. The XR world is a simulation of real-world behaviors, with added superpowers for the user.

Because the user lives in that world, they have high expectations, deeply embedded in the brain's limbic system, on how things should be. Anything that departs from the learnings of human evolution has to be an obvious benefit, shortcut, or superpower, to be accepted. That includes visual consistency, style reference, scale, and believability. Spatial audio and especially narrative audio have played a big role in VR experiences, because they are relatively easy to produce and offer a great way to navigate a user through an XR world. Orientation problems, interaction guidance, and onboarding very often rely heavily on audio narration because it is performance-friendly, easy to produce and implement. It is the low-hanging fruit of XR design, because it can accomplish a lot with very little effort. A good number of XR titles rely heavily on extensive XR narration, giving hints, guidance, and navigation notifications, on top of the storytelling layer.

Voice navigation on the other hand, such as voice commands and voice search, is also becoming increasingly important in XR, for the obvious reason that text input using controllers is often tedious and time consuming. Voice navigation is used in applications like *Wander* on the Oculus Quest, to quickly input a desired destination, and it has been part of the MRTK showcase, to demonstrate how voice can assist, when both hands are busy, with scrolling through a map. In this case, voice input is used for "zoom in" and "zoom out" commands, resulting in a dramatic increase of productivity. With the importance of spatial audio in immersive XR, voice seems to be a natural extension in the dialog with a digital environment.

Touch, mostly experienced through controller vibration, is experienced in a much more subtle way. Nevertheless, it is an important interaction signal to communicate to the user if an item has been selected or activated, is overlapping with scene geometry, or is doing something important or unwanted. It brings the user's attention to the controller interaction and signals that there is an interaction result. Touch or vibration is a subtle but important part of a satisfying user experience; it enhances the sensual input with a physical attribute.

4.4.1 XR Interaction Design and the OODA Loop

In a qualitative survey for this book, to examine how designers plan, conceptualize, and design a digital XR product, it became clear that a good number of XR designers have their own unique methods or in-house procedures to tackle a production.

It is often a good idea to have more than one strategy up your sleeve if confronted with urgent, time-sensitive, rushed, complicated, and impossible productions. Traditionally, product designers in the XR field follow game production standards, producing a live game design document (GDD) as the centerpiece of the production.

One experienced XR designer, who has a number of successful titles under his belt, pointed out that he uses a method called the OODA loop in his game design process. The OODA loop is a four-step approach (observe, orient, decide, act) to decision making and was developed by military strategist John Boyd for the combat operations process. The concept has been used in game design as a competitive decision-making tool. It is a way to quickly process incoming information and make intelligent decisions (Figure 4-8).

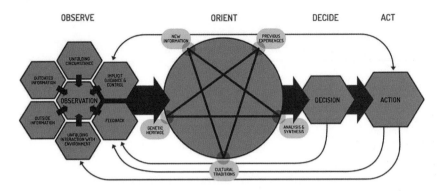

Figure 4-8. *The OODA loop (image by C. Hillmann)*

An XR experience or game can be seen as a sequence of player-enacted decisions. In the OODA loop, the first "observe" stage is all about data. The user is observing the available resources and collecting the data.

"Orient" is the stage where they take action to assign meaning to the collected data and where they eliminate unnecessary data chunks. At the "decide" stage, they evaluate the risks and rewards and prioritize before entering engagement, based on their persona. During the "act" stage, the user executes their plan and changes the state of the situation with their behavior.

An XR title or game can be evaluated based on these four stages, in case the user runs into recurring problems during the experience.

For example, if the user fails to take advantage of a helpful feature, the problem may be the misreading of presented information at the "observe" stage. Or, if users tend to take only one of many possible options, the problem could be at the "decide" stage, when the available options are not presented clearly enough.

The OODA loop is a concept to detect problems in a digital product. It can be used as a framework to strategically go after user errors and less-than-optimal outcomes of a XR experience or game design. The OODA loop has not only been an important concept in military strategy and law enforcement, but has also been adapted by businesses and the public sector, most notably for cybersecurity. It is a helpful addition to the UX design toolbox, to analyze user behavior and eliminate unwanted results and user errors.

4.4.2 The GDD and XR Interaction Design

The centerpiece of game design is the game design document (GDD). A GDD is really a specialized product design document, because games are digital products that are complicated to make, including its art production pipeline, creative design dependencies, and the scope of its technical requirements. A GDD is special in every sense; it not only represents every aspect and production detail of the product's vision, but it also often reflects the cultural context and history of its colorful industry. Product design for mobile and web applications does not require a design document to be the central focal point, because design and development are very clearly separated before and after the developer handoff. Not so in game design, because the scope and the production dependencies require it.

The fact that XR experiences often fall into the game category makes this an important part of the design process. Even XR experiences that are not obviously, or primarily, games very often have game-like characteristics that make a GDD a necessity. In that sense we could speak of an XR design document, an XRDD, which would have the exact same characteristics as a GDD. But it probably makes it easier to continue using the term GDD, because everyone understands what it is. Interactive design, navigation components, storytelling, and backstory, as well as demographics and marketing considerations, are all part of a GDD and often form the backbone of a production with a living document, shared by developers, designers, and stakeholders. Agile game design documentation, based on a live GDD, helps to maintain a vision of the final product, providing detailed descriptions regarding game objectives and progressions as well as game mechanics and elements (Figure 4-9).

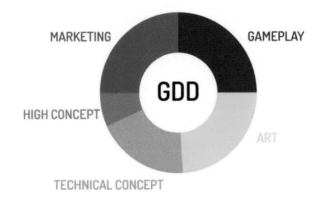

Figure 4-9. *The GDD (image by C. Hillmann)*

The GDD consists of an established structure that has evolved over decades of successful game productions. It overlaps in many areas with the digital product design tasks of a UX designer conceptualizing an interactive experience. It covers details of the targeted demographic and their specific preferences. It documents the user flow and storytelling and specifies the user interaction, information architecture, and visual language, plus technical requirements, assets, and project scope.

GDDs are also a reflection of gaming culture. A number of GDDs from successful games are publicly available and can be studied by aspiring game designers. The document often reflects the spirit and vision of the final game, its genre and culture, in the presentation style and its choice of illustrations, fonts, and iconography. The GDD is more than just a technical documentation; it is also a motivational tool and a resource to keep the team and stakeholders on the same page.

The sections of a GDD are typically as follows:

1. The executive summary with game concept, concept art, target demographic, genre, and scope of production

2. Game structure: Describing game objectives and progressions, including levels and features

3. Game mechanics: Interaction concept, game mechanics, UI

4. Backstory: Narrative, storytelling, and characters

5. Sound, music, and art asset listing

6. Technical considerations: Targeted platforms, game engines, middleware, and production pipeline

7. Marketing and funding: Budget, monetization, advertising, and promotion

The GDD is typically the heart of a game production and its descriptive format the most important source of information for level designers, artists, and developers. The majority of sections in a GDD carry over to any XR production, even when it is an enterprise project or an XR product exploration app for a promotional event.

In a lot of cases, the XR GDD will be stripped of its deep game considerations on backstory, characters, and so forth, while the main objective stays the same: to give an overview over the goals, requirements, and scope of a project.

With regard to the double diamond and the process of OOUX mapping, in our example called the Reality UX process, the XR GDD is updated with product details, including an asset list, after the OOUX XR mapping has been completed.

At this point, such product questions as what needs to be designed for whom have been narrowed down; its mental models have been translated into OOUX; and the outcome, the actual objects required for the prototype, has been defined and captured in the asset list of the XR GDD. The next step to follow is the production of a prototype to test and iterate.

The GDD is the document that captures the results of the double diamond and, as an agile document, is dynamically updated when new data, such as testing results, become available.

Compared to the conventional computer game GDD, the XR GDD has to cover a number of additional parameters unique to immersive media, such as comfort considerations, stereoscopic depth consistency, and game mechanics that rely on spatial components, for example, 360 audio cues.

The GDD for a computer game is typically created after an innovative idea, a genre inspiration, or an iteration of an existing game, followed by building out the structure, backstory, and level concepts to give an overview over all aspects of the endeavor to produce such a project. The process to kick-start an XR GDD is often very different if it follows the UX double diamond approach, typically for non-gaming titles. The double diamond approach is used to find a solution for a problem. Once the right solution has been found, it is then translated into the language of an XR production using the XR GDD to reflect all components necessary. The second half of the double diamond is reflected in the dynamic change of the GDD, as new prototypes are built and updated test data result in design iterations.

4.5 XR and Mindful Design

The concept of mindful design emerged at first in the 2000s, but has only recently risen to major prominence. This development was not only partially a reaction to concerns over dark pattern/manipulative design but also a result of general unease concerning media overconsumption and addiction and unhealthy user behavior in the context of social media.

Mindful design has the potential to be very important for XR design, considering the potential problems of immersive media, once it finds wider mainstream adoption.

Mindful design philosophy is user oriented and focuses on behavioral change, responsible design decisions, and awareness over health and safety issues the user may encounter, issues that will become more important in the XR space over time.

A good example is the screen time feature of Apple's iOS. The application allows the user to be mindful about their own media consumption habits and gives access to tools that enable the user to monitor possible unhealthy behavior. By enabling the feature, users can monitor their own media usage on cloud-connected iOS devices and view the corresponding data analytics broken down into app use by day or week. It allows users to review their own media behavior and make adjustments and set limits, if they consider the consumption to be too high.

Similar features are also available on Android and third-party apps.

Another good example of mindful design is to respect the user's privacy and offer transparency over sharing and data usage, plus easy access to control the settings that concern user data.

Digital well-being is an important part of the long-term-user experience. If a product is successful, it is typically used a lot (i.e., heavy usage is a metric for measuring regarded as a success of a digital product). However, the potential side effect or flip side of a heavily used product is often easily overlooked and might not be on the radar from the business perspective. Nevertheless, there are enough reasons for user well-being, when using a digital product, to be part of a long-term business goal, to avoid unhealthy behavior resulting in rapid behavioral changes, including quitting the usage altogether. The lessons learned during the rise of mobile gaming and social media are important for immersive media, as XR experiences have the potential to be even more harmful, addictive, and disruptive to family life, if not properly kept in check by mindful design principles (Figure 4-10).

Figure 4-10. *Mindful design and its context (image by C. Hillmann)*

UX designers embracing mindful design usually implement mindful design features in the user's interaction, onboarding, and notification features.

Typical areas for mindful design concerns are as follows:

– Balancing family life and technology

– Unplugging more often

– Parental controls

– Setting usage limits

– Allowing easy access to privacy and data sharing options

– Paying attention to inclusion, diversity, and accessibility

Another area of mindful design is stepping beyond these practical implementations and tying the user's behavior into larger issues of environmental concern, such as reducing energy consumption, waste, and

CO^2 emission or the recyclability of products. Even though an XR device, or digital product, is not a primary suspect for environmental damage, awareness and sustainability efforts can be brought into experience areas where they seem fit, for example, in travel destination experiences or product exploration experiences for related fields such as transport, shipping, and energy consumption, in general.

Immersive media is often seen as an escapist medium; therefore, it is a good idea to counterbalance the perception with awareness campaigns and nonprofit support, whenever the subject matter allows it.

As XR adoption in society is growing over the years, we will see more concerns over mental health issues, especially for vulnerable demographics. People with underlying depression and anxiety, and addictive personalities, will be especially sensitive to the cognitive load from an immersive experience. A lot can be learned from the well-studied field of gaming addiction, which is now a recognized disorder by the World Health Organization (classified as "gaming disorder"). Game addiction is well documented, with a wide field of academic research, case studies, and support organizations available to tap into.

It is a good future-proof strategy for immersive media and digital XR applications to take digital well-being seriously as the mainstream adoption of XR products grows and potential issues may arise.

4.6 Summary

This chapter looked at the evolution of UX design in the 3D space and the pain point for user interaction. It evaluated the double diamond UX design process using an object-oriented approach and looked at a custom design problem-solving concept called Reality UX. The chapter looked at the OODA loop as a way to manage a project and the GDD as the foundation of game design. Finally, it examined digital heath and mindful design as important subjects for the future of XR.

CHAPTER 5

Pioneering Platforms and UX Learnings

5.1 Introduction

This chapter looks at the pioneering platforms, prototyping tools, and tech trends for XR applications and evaluates what UX learnings can be brought forward from the leading formats of the industry. How can UX designers prototype XR interaction with efficiency? What are the applications and tools to test ideas, and which core concepts have been established to improve digital XR products and bring immersive concepts to life?

Prototyping is the bread and butter of UX design, and it takes different forms in the XR field—prototyping as used for ideation, to develop ideas and pitch them to stakeholders, business partners, or potential clients, or to prototype, test, and iterate. In XR these are often two separate processes: The low-fidelity ideation prototype can start with a script, a scribble, a 3D mockup, or a concept presented with a dedicated XR prototyping application, as opposed to the high-fidelity iteration prototype, which has to be a functional, interactive version of the concept, made with a game engine and is intended for user testing.

The transition between a low-fidelity to a high-fidelity prototype is seamless for web and mobile maps, but not so in XR, at least not yet. The gap between these two stages of prototyping will become narrower as the

© Cornel Hillmann 2021
C. Hillmann, *UX for XR*, https://doi.org/10.1007/978-1-4842-7020-2_5

industry matures and toolsets become more accessible and easier to use. A number of prototyping tools are rapidly progressing toward the goal to make the process seamless. For example, an XR ideation prototype with Microsoft Marquette can be directly exported to the Unity game engine, to add interactivity and functions only available within a game engine framework. In that sense, Marquette and its tools provide a path from ideation to testing and the final XR product. In other instances, the ideation process is a separate stage to sketch out ideas with a low-fidelity concept, while the actual high-fidelity iteration prototype for testing is built from scratch using an XR framework in Unreal or Unity, providing core functions for XR interactions (Figure 5-1).

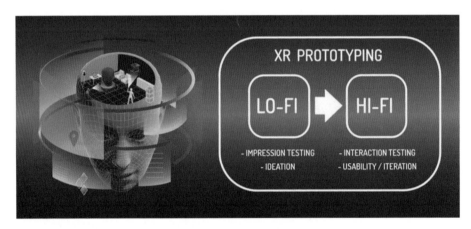

Figure 5-1. *XR prototyping: low-fidelity ideation vs. high-fidelity iteration prototype (image by C. Hillmann)*

The prototyping process, as part of the UX design approach, is particularly important for non-gaming XR applications, because of users without prior XR exposure and specific requirements or KPIs that require usability testing and analysis. The success of highly specialized XR applications relies on UX to guarantee user acceptance. XR has already carved out a niche in a number of key industries. The fact is a good amount of niche XR solutions don't get a lot of visibility, even though they do provide measurable value to their industries. The success stories are often circulated within VR professional newsletters or on specialized enterprise platforms such as "Oculus for Business." Case studies published there, for example, showcase breakthrough business solutions using Oculus technology, to give these innovative use cases more visibility and demonstrate that there is much more to XR than gaming and leisure. One recent example in an Oculus business report was the solution by Nanome.ai, helping Nimbus Therapeutics, a biotechnology company for selective small molecule therapeutics, by using their virtual reality solution for molecular modeling (Figure 5-2).

Figure 5-2. *Oculus Quest 2 user with Nanome for molecular design (image by C. Hillmann)*

Nanome is one of many successful examples for a highly specialized XR solution in a narrow business field, with very little public visibility. The targeted users are medicinal chemists, structural biologists, and biotech engineers, who may not be familiar with VR gaming conventions and require special attention to onboarding instructions and comfort considerations.

Non-gaming XR applications for consumers still live in a niche, as well, but are constantly growing, as we can see with product tryout apps using handheld AR, superimposing a digital product on the environment (furniture, art) or on the user (fashion, accessories, tattoos) to evaluate a purchase. Besides the success of XR in education and especially in fitness, like the success of the VR fitness platform Holofit (Figure 5-3), the next generation of VR-enabled ecommerce applications such as VResorts Booking (vresorts.io) are still at the early stages of testing on the SideQuest platform.

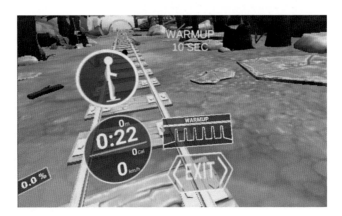

Figure 5-3. *VR fitness with Holofit*

VResorts Booking is based on the idea that an immersive presentation during the booking process will enhance and stimulate the user's decision-making process to purchase a luxury vacation. The ability to pre-experience the hotel and destination appears to be the logical next step in the evolution of leisure travel ecommerce (Figure 5-4).

Figure 5-4. *Immersive vacation browsing with VResorts Booking*

Building a successful digital product for the next generation of XR-enabled ecommerce applications, as well as XR business solutions in highly specialized enterprise segments, requires prototyping and user testing as a critical part of the UX design process. Prototyping, testing, and iterating a design is just as important in XR as in web and mobile applications, but the prototyping process is often much more complex.

XR prototyping tools are available for all XR platforms, but vary in the degree of learning curve and features. The ultimate goal for a UX designer is to evaluate a concept with a fully interactive high-fidelity prototype at the important testing stage. Some prototyping tools are primarily focused on ideation and sketching out the visual storytelling concept, while other prototyping solution tools provide the elements to build interactivity, often through visual scripting capabilities. Let's have a look at the pioneering solutions, platform tools, and UX learnings, with a focus on the industry leaders and their toolsets.

5.2 Handheld AR Breakthroughs

One of the industry leaders in handheld AR is without a doubt Adobe Inc. The company has built a wide-reaching ecosystem for digital business and design solutions across iOS and Android platforms, and it has put forward a strong commitment to the future of AR with its authoring and publishing tool, Adobe Aero, which is part of the company's AR strategy and wider 3D vertical that includes applications such as Mixamo and Substance Painter. Adobe Aero is a user-friendly approach to designing AR interactivity, and the platform's creations can be easily shared with a link or QR code, provided the recipient has the Aero app installed. Beside its main use case as a tool to create Aero AR experiences, it can also be used to prototype AR object interaction before building a high-fidelity handheld AR prototype with Unity or Unreal. Adobe Aero integrates with the innovative character animation tool Mixamo that Adobe acquired in 2015. Mixamo is used widely by the indie game development community, because it provides an easy way to automatically rig a 3D character and set it up with a variety of standard game character motions. Together with Substance Painter, the industry-leading PBR texturing tool for 3D game assets, Adobe provides a solid lineup for 3D content creation to empower ideation and look development targeting handheld AR platforms.

Using Aero for look development and ideation prototyping is accessible and straightforward. Evaluating how a 3D design can be brought to life within a spatial storytelling context is the core strength of the tool. Aero enables the UX designer to try out ideas and get feedback with user testing, before committing to any platform, technology, or framework. Typically, these are focused on individual AR object activation and not on AR inventory applications in the "product tryout"–type category, such as the often-quoted IKEA *Place* app.

5.2.1 Spatial Storytelling with Adobe Aero

Adobe Aero enables designers to build interactive AR scenes with an intuitive mobile app and an extended desktop version that offers additional tools to build object behaviors. The final output is targeting three AR anchor types: horizontal surface, vertical surface, and image (Figure 5-5).

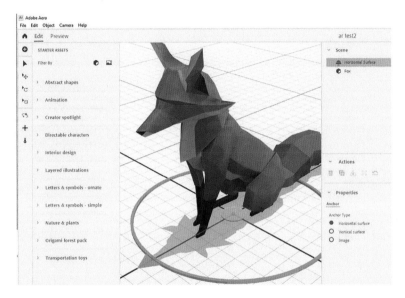

Figure 5-5. *Adobe Aero anchor types (right-hand panel)*

These three types reflect the most common use cases when AR scenes are shared, for example, an AR scene that plays out on the user's tabletop; a vertical AR scene, targeting a wall in proximity of the user; or a predefined image, very often a marker in a book or magazine, the wall art of an exhibition, or mural. Aero comes with a library of ready-to-use assets, including a directable character that can be moved toward a pin, after activation (Figure 5-6).

Figure 5-6. *The "move to" behavior targeting the scene pin "pin1"*

Each scene item can get an individual trigger by selecting from start, tap, and proximity. The behavior builder is then used to design a sequence of actions to follow in sequence after the activation. Aero's features are focused on the most common use cases for sharable AR scenes. It enables designers to construct micro-stories using multiple behavior building blocks, typically with the goal to reveal an announcement or URL, for example, a scene where a character walks over to the next, waiting for tab activation. Once tab is activated, the animation and audio message are played, and the character reveals their animated audio message to finally open a URL (Figure 5-7).

Figure 5-7. *Building micro-stories: setting behaviors for two Aero characters*

Character interaction is just one of many possible ways to build an AR scene with Aero. Very often, designers use complex motion graphics to reach out with a shareable AR object, whose interactive behavior has been brought to life with the Aero desktop application, using animated 3D assets or motion graphics.

5.2.2 3D Tools of the AR Trade

While Aero is used to compose an AR scene and design its behaviors, the 3D design, texturing, and animation is typically done with digital content creation (DCC) tools. Popular with indie game developers is Blender 3D, while specialized motion designers often prefer Cinema 4D for its motion graphics features and the tight integration with Adobe products. Look development and texturing are often done with Adobe Substance Painter or Marmoset Toolbag, especially if the final product relies heavily on PBR materials (Figure 5-8).

Figure 5-8. *Look development with Marmoset Toolbag*

One of the most important aspects of an AR object is often the animation. The AR object animation is typically used to signal if an item is waiting for activation using an idle animation loop, or it reveals the AR story segments through its motion design. Because animation plays such a central role in the interaction design that brings the AR magic to life, designers often use specialized tools such as Nukeygara Akeytsu to keyframe animation loops that blend convincingly into each other.

Akeytsu's strength is the focus on game animation, as it provides skeleton presets for both the Unreal and Unity game engines, and its workflow is specialized on animation loops, ease of use, and efficiency in the motion design process (Figure 5-9).

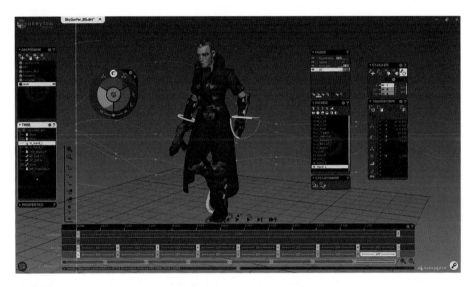

Figure 5-9. *Character animation and motion design for XR using Akeytsu*

A typical AR production pipeline would go like this: designing a 3D asset in Blender, look development and texturing in Marmoset Toolbag or Substance Painter, and 3D object animation in Akeytsu, before bringing it into Adobe Aero to assign behaviors and animation triggers. The final output or AR object prototype can then be shared with a link or a QR code for user testing.

Adobe Aero has a sharp focus on very common use cases for handheld AR, and, as an industry heavyweight, Adobe has shown its commitment to the AR evolution. If the Aero platform continues to grow its user base, it will become one of the industry standards for spatial storytelling in AR. The fact that a majority of creative professionals are already committed to the Adobe ecosystem makes this scenario a likely outcome.

5.2.3 Social Media AR

Next to the powerhouse Adobe are the leading social media platforms that are pioneering the handheld AR field. The social media messaging innovator Snapchat has been a leader in AR since its early days a decade ago. Its free creator tool Lens Studio provides a sophisticated development environment to deliver the rich AR interactions for which Snapchat is famous. Not only has Snapchat been leading the way with the visual quality of its features but the company is also spearheading innovation with cutting-edge AR features such as full-body motion tracking. One of the reasons Snapchat is becoming a destination for visual storytellers is the feature-rich AR production suite that Lens Studio provides, including a visual scripting editor to design complex behaviors (Figure 5-10).

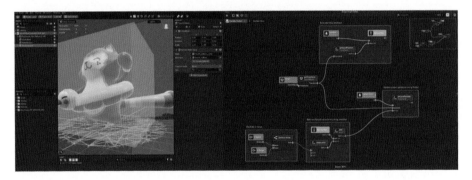

Figure 5-10. *Lens Studio material editor and visual scripting*

Spark AR Studio by Facebook has a similar concept, targeting AR overlays for its Facebook and Instagram social media platforms. While the software is mostly associated with AR face overlay filters, it also has a capable object editor to place AR objects in the user's environment using templates for 2D and 3D stickers. An innovative option to test a Spark AR object's interaction with the environment is the Spark AR Player for the Oculus Quest. The VR app, available via the Oculus App Lab preview channel, simulates a smartphone user's environment in virtual reality.

By choosing from a selection of mobile devices, plus environment and lighting settings, an imported Spark AR project can be experienced in the VR viewer for testing. The connection between Spark AR Studio on a desktop PC and the Spark AR Player in VR is wireless and instant, allowing for a quick evaluation of ideas and look development iterations. As a timesaver and shortcut for XR look development, we will most likely see more of these kinds of synergies and productivity tools between AR and VR applications (Figure 5-11).

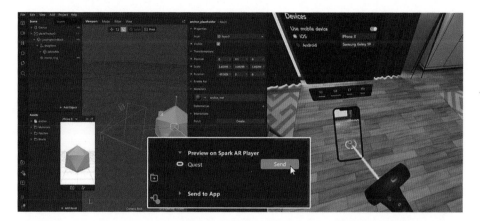

Figure 5-11. *Sending a Spark AR Studio project (left) directly to the Oculus Quest (right) for testing*

5.2.4 The Handheld AR Landscape

Next to Adobe and the social media giants, we have a constantly changing landscape of AR solutions from such apps as Blippar and Zappar that allow brands to build AR marketing experiences with easy-to-use creation tools. These tools typically are focused on image marker and QR code–activated, handheld AR experiences and require a creator subscription.

EyeJack is an example of a highly focused handheld AR application targeting the curation and distribution of AR art and has become a popular use case for events. The subscription-based EyeJack creator app makes it easy to add design layers to an image marker to trigger animated effects. It is an effective method to overlay animated versions of a static wall art piece—and a tool to add a digital storytelling layer to an exhibition or event.

The Unreal and Unity engines both support Apple's ARKit and Google's ARCore. Unity does this through its AR foundation API and a dedicated solution to environment sensor data, called Unity MARS, a subscription-based AR development toolset. In addition to that, the Unity asset store provides a number of third-party solutions for AR, most notably the AR platform Vuforia. Vuforia is a widely used AR engine with Unity integration. It is subscription based but free to use as a watermarked demo and allows designers to quickly prototype concepts for image marker–based AR applications with accessible and easy-to-use features (Figure 5-12).

Figure 5-12. *Vuforia in the Unity asset store*

The advantage of the Unreal engine, on the other hand, is its unified AR tool suite with a platform-agnostic approach for the most common AR features and supported by the powerful Blueprints visual scripting system that allows designers to quickly prototype ideas without coding. Similar to Unity, a number of special AR frameworks and toolsets are available in the Unreal marketplace to kick-start the design process (Figure 5-13).

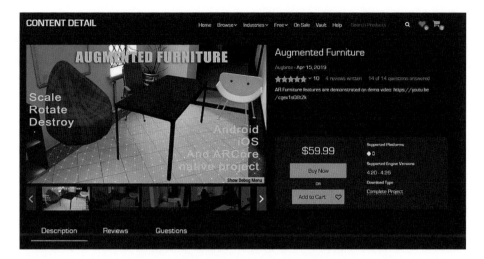

Figure 5-13. *Augmented furniture toolkit in the Unreal marketplace*

Designing handheld AR interactions has become more user-friendly, for example, with the inclusion of Apple's AR creation tool Reality Composer as part of the Xcode toolkit. The visual 3D environment gives designers options to position virtual objects in the scene and add animations, triggered sounds, and behaviors driven by physics simulation. A composition can be exported as a lightweight .reality or .usdz file in an Apple Quick Look experience for impression testing.

More complex handheld AR often requires an app or a social media platform to view a shared AR object and experience its interaction behaviors, with the notable exception of WebAR. Most modern browsers support WebAR, hence making this the most accessible platform because a web browser comes preinstalled with the system. WebAR is developing at a rapid pace, and companies such as Blippar.com, Zappar.com, and 8thwall. com provide the toolkits for developers and designers to build the next generation of WebAR-enabled applications.

5.2.5 Handheld AR UX

What are the AR interaction features to keep an eye on, and what opportunities of handheld AR (HAR) need to be considered for prototyping? For one, the handheld AR experience is centered around the device's camera and the superimposed virtual objects, requiring a few base rules and considerations for a successful user experience (Figure 5-14).

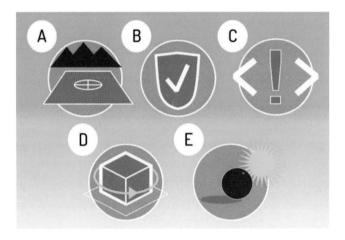

Figure 5-14. *Basic handheld AR concepts: (a) Environment context, (b) comfort and safety, (c) off-screen cues, (d) object interaction, (e) scene light and materials (image by C. Hillmann)*

a) Environment context: The user's environment is central to the experience. It is important to communicate the environment requirements and possibly offer feature options for different kinds of environment settings.

b) Comfort and safety: It is important to guide the user with onboarding, coaching, and safety instructions that include reminding immersed users of their physical environment, for example, when doing rapid motions.

Comfort for handheld AR is just as essential. A handheld mobile device is only comfortable to hold in position, or at a certain angle, for a limited amount of time. Options to engage the users with extended content that doesn't require handheld AR interaction bring variety to the experience. For example, a virtual item can be picked up in the spatial AR environment, but becomes available for exploration without AR thereafter.

c) Off-screen cues: Left and right arrows help the user to discover content that is currently off-screen.

d) Object interaction: Using direct controls with familiar gestures, 3D hints, and visual indicators for more information makes the interaction intuitive. Simplicity, for example, using the entire display with minimal use of text, but including vibration haptics and audio effects for interaction events, enhances the experience.

e) Considering the AR object's lighting, shadows, and reflective surfaces is an important part in communicating object properties and relative positions in the user's environment. AR object shadows give cues over surface distances and whether virtual items are grounded, attached, or floating.

Most handheld AR development tools support wearable AR as an optional target platform. This option brings on the question of responsiveness toward device categories. A handheld AR device is typically positioned at below shoulder height, while AR glasses display at eyeline height. The content may have to be adjusted regarding the viewing distance and to take advantage of the stereoscopic depth sensing of AR headsets.

5.3 VR: The Oculus Ecosystem

Oculus is currently dominating the consumer VR market and, at the time of writing this book, the Oculus Quest 2 is the most used headset on Steam. Next to its consumer and games focus, the platform has built an impressive ecosystem of creative, productivity, and development tools that can help UX designers with ideation, prototyping, testing, and team communications.

5.3.1 Ideation, Grayboxing, and Early Prototyping

An important part in the VR UX design process is ideation in VR. A VR concept may look good on paper, but only when experienced immersed in the virtual world will it actually reveal how well the 3D concept contributes to the bigger idea of the experience. Sketching out a 3D concept in VR, blocking out its basic components and depth layers, helps to communicate the design vision at an early stage. The lineup of creative tools supporting Oculus headsets has grown over the years. Most tools allow geometry creation and surface coloring, while some apps support sculpting and others come with asset libraries. Between the applications that are native on the Oculus Quest and applications that require a PC, but are accessible with an Oculus Link connection, Gravity Sketch stands out as a professional product design tool, with features to create complex organic shapes, including subdivision surfaces (Figure 5-15).

Figure 5-15. *Grayboxing with Gravity Sketch using the Oculus Quest*

Grayboxing, a common game-level design technique, means blocking out ideas with untextured geometry, before getting too much into surface detail and refined environment assets. It is a way to test out how a 3D space can be used for an experience, what items are placed in front, which backdrop will be used, and how the layout affects playability. It is also a way to do impression testing, by presenting ideas to users and stakeholders to get early feedback on ideas.

Creative applications Google Tilt Brush and Adobe Medium are focused on immersive art creation, which can also be used to sketch out a VR experience. Oculus Quill, on the other hand, has a focus on storytelling with animations and camera positions. It is a capable solution to conceptualize a VR narrative with animations and audio for impression testing.

Next to general modeling and creative tools, a dedicated prototyping tool such as Tvori, available as a PC version via Oculus Link or a standalone native Quest version, currently in Beta, has clear advantages when addressing the design of UI elements (Figure 5-16).

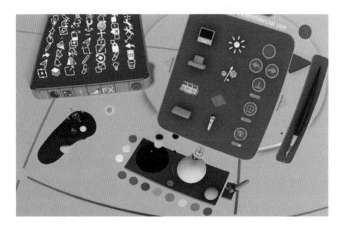

Figure 5-16. *Prototyping using the Tvori UI asset library and the Oculus Quest*

Tvori provides a number of asset packs helping with typical UX/UI work for XR. Curved menu screen, UI objects, and 2D UI icon libraries provide a solution for rapid prototyping in VR using pre-made content packs. The pro and enterprise versions enable export to a standalone version or the Oculus viewer app. Tvori is one of a number of applications focused on prototyping and design collaboration. Like other XR prototyping solutions as Microsoft Marquette, it does not yet provide tools to build interaction logic within the application; instead, it is intended for visualization, ideation, look development, and impression testing, during the first prototyping phase.

5.3.2 Frameworks and Tools

Building prototypes that include interaction logic requires a framework based on the Unity or Unreal game engine. Instead of building standard interaction modules and locomotion options from scratch, these frameworks provide the essential interaction elements as pre-build components that can be customized or extended using visual scripting tools such as Blueprints with Unreal or Bolt with Unity. One example for a sophisticated VR framework is the Advanced VR Framework by Humancodeable.org for the Unreal engine. The framework provides a modular and extensible concept, targeting VR presentation, architectural visualizations, training, product demos, and games. The solution comes as a configurable component-based system applicable for PC and standalone VR devices, covering object interaction, navigation, dynamic user interfaces, and multiplayer options, providing the essential building blocks for rapid prototyping and testing (Figure 5-17).

Figure 5-17. *Framework feature Tiny Display for grabbed objects in the Advanced VR Framework for UE4 by Human Codeable (Humancodeable.org)*

Unity provides an *XR interaction toolkit* with the engine that provides basic unified AR/VR interaction components for object interaction, UI interaction, and locomotion. While these building blocks provide a good starting point, there are also commercial options with a larger variety of interaction types as an alternative to the previously popular open source VRTK and specialized toolkits for hand interaction, such as the Hand Tracking Interaction Builder by LayerCakeDesign. The VR Interaction Framework by Bearded Ninja Games is one of the most complete VR frameworks for the Unity engine targeting VR headsets. It provides a broad range of specific interaction components, including curved UI integration, climbing, and 3D markers, among other specialized components (Figure 5-18).

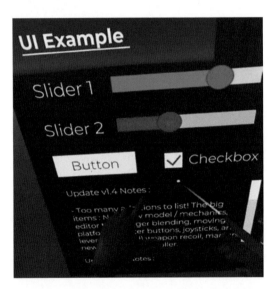

Figure 5-18. *UI example in the VR Interaction Framework by Bearded Ninja Games for Unity*

Despite the learning curve, it is often a good idea to become familiar with at least one of the leading frameworks, so as to be able to quickly test interactions and sketch out ideas that are fully interactive. Frameworks are typically a starting point, while the engine's visual scripting environment provides the tools to expand the provided elements with custom-built functions.

Testing an interactive VR concept is pretty straightforward. Oculus provides a convenient companion tool called Oculus Developer Hub. One of the features is the option to capture a screen recording on the linked PC, a setup that can help when testing users' experiences during the prototyping and iterative process. By conveniently monitoring and testing a user's experience, UX designers can execute qualitative surveys with test participants to get insights and user feedback.

Another way to get feedback on a prototype is to publish an early access version on SideQuest, Steam, or the Oculus App Lab. These platforms are alternatives to the official Oculus store, with very high entry requirements for developers. One example is Triangle Factory's Hyper Dash multiplayer VR shooter that was developed while receiving feedback from its community on the SideQuest platform, before the game was officially released on the Oculus store. An alternative for smaller projects, for example, product explorations for events, is to develop a WebVR version first and obtain feedback by distributing the WebVR link. The nonprofit, open source organization Mozilla has released a WebXR Exporter package for Unity that simplifies the process of deploying a VR concept to WebVR-supporting browsers, allowing to iterate ideas on a device-agnostic platform. Most modern browsers support WebVR, including the integrated Oculus browser, of course.

Part of the Oculus ecosystem are the many collaboration and meeting platforms that became essentially important during the Covid-19 pandemic in 2020 and increasingly popular for international projects with team members across different continents. The private VR team meetup platforms—Bigscreen, Altspace, and Mozilla Hubs—are on the more casual side, while more enterprise-oriented solutions like Arthur.digital and Spatial.io offer additional productivity tools, such as whiteboards and asset imports. VR team meetups will continue to grow as an important part of design collaborations in the future. A VR meetup can provide an alternative to a Zoom meeting, for example, bringing a 3D object into the session as part of a design review during the look development phase (Figure 5-19).

Figure 5-19. *Creating a Post-it note in a virtual team meeting using Spatial.io*

5.4 Microsoft HoloLens: Entertain, Inform, Assist, and Inspire

Augmented reality wearables are currently focused on the enterprise market. Pioneering headset developer Magic Leap, which was originally targeting the consumer market, has pivoted to enterprise, due to the better business environment. The refocus on enterprise XR was necessary because the technology was still too expensive to gain meaningful consumer traction outside of industrial use, including engineering, warehousing, and corporate communication.

Microsoft has been targeting the enterprise world since the release of its first HoloLens development edition in 2016. When the HoloLens 2 was released in February 2019, it already had an impressive lineup of enterprise partners (Figure 5-20). The HoloLens 2 was a major breakthrough in many UX-related areas, most notably, display, comfort, and interaction quality.

Figure 5-20. *AR headset UI interaction (image by C. Hillmann)*

Microsoft is clearly spearheading the AR field with its developer community, *mixed-reality* ecosystem, and road map that includes Azure spatial anchors, as persistent digital objects in the AR cloud and a multiuser mixed-reality platform called Microsoft Mesh. Sophisticated toolkits, such as the Mixed Reality Toolkit (MRTK), reflect the experience and maturity of the development and design environment.

The technology has come to the point when it will soon spill into the consumer market. It is simply a matter of time and price point. For that reason, game developers, media platforms, and consumer brands are experimenting with their tools, so as to be ready when this transition happens.

5.4.1 The Vision: A Mixed-Reality Mirror World with Azure Spatial Anchors and Microsoft Mesh

When Microsoft acquired the struggling social VR pioneer AltspaceVR in 2017, hardly anyone suspected that this takeover would play a key role in Microsoft vision for a multiuser VR cloud. Announced in March 2021 during a VR keynote held in Altspace, HoloLens lead developer Alex Kipman showcased the vision of social VR and its infrastructure. Microsoft has been rebuilding Altspace using Mesh and intends to offer enterprise sections to their clients, using its key features, such as privacy, security, and integration with data, AI, and *mixed-reality* services.

This upgrade of AltspaceVR will also benefit consumers and professionals who have been using Altspace as a VR meetup and event space. AltspaceVR is expected to be one of the major showcases of Microsoft Mesh and its features. Since its early days in 2013, AltspaceVR has earned its reputation as a social VR destination that delivers substantial value to its users through entertainment events, such as stand-up comedy nights, live music, dance parties, as well as professional workshops and discussion groups. The platform gained a lot of respect for its virtual version of the iconic Burning Man gathering in 2020, when the physical event in Nevada had to be canceled because of the pandemic.

Microsoft's XR ecosystem, branded Mixed Reality, supports both VR and AR, but the HoloLens stands out as a groundbreaking product, trailblazing the industry in terms of quality, features, and tools. The backbone, Microsoft's cloud service Azure, delivers the infrastructure for AR's persistent digital objects: a mirror world that locks bytes to atoms and digital data to physical space and thus provides the environment to build a multiuser digital world with spatial anchors. The benefit of the mirror world is to have a digital twin, a virtual representation of physical places, to provide data interfaces with connected systems, the Internet of Things (IoT), and spatial location data provided by a geographic information system (GIS). It's a future-oriented XR development vision for a wide range of industries, government services, and consumer applications. As previously mentioned, Microsoft is not alone; the spatial computing infrastructure, often called mirror world, is also pursued by Apple, Google, and Facebook, among others (Figure 5-21).

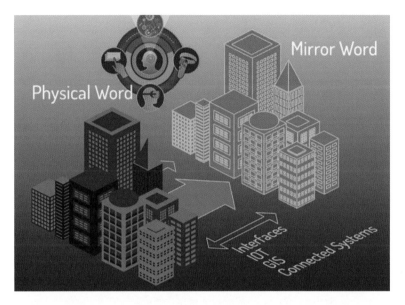

Figure 5-21. *Design thinking for the Metaverse, also called a mirror world, or digital twin of the real-world (image by C. Hillmann)*

5.4.2 Prototyping with Microsoft Marquette

Microsoft's Mixed Reality prototyping tool Marquette has been made available to Oculus Link PC users via a Steam version. It is a feature-rich and free XR application targeting ideation and mixed-reality mockups, including the ability to export a Marquette concept to Unity with a dedicated plugin. This workflow allows UX designers to sketch out a mockup of interface and screen components and export it to Unity, where the actual interaction logic can be applied with Unity's visual scripting tool Bolt, among others. Marquette can work with imported geometry and features a wide variety of UI objects, text and line tools to design visual interaction concepts and XR scene layouts. It is an excellent starting point to communicate ideas at the early stage to get stakeholder or user feedback with impression testing. It is also a very comprehensive starting point to pitch an XR solution to a client with an immersive mockup (Figure 5-22).

Figure 5-22. *Ideation and mockups for XR with Microsoft Marquette*

A typical Microsoft Marquette workflow is to test an AR concept in a VR environment by importing a representative 3D room mockup as a backdrop. The big idea is to "design in context" and test 3D elements from the immersive user perspective. Immersive design enables a direct approach in conceptualizing an XR scene. It allows to test the 3D offset of

UI elements and enables object parallax testing as well as UI typography evaluation, by being there in VR and feeling it as the user would. The alternative to prototyping in VR using Marquette or any other prototyping tool, such as Tvori, is to design a complete 3D mockup in a 3D software with basic VR support, such as Blender (Figure 5-23).

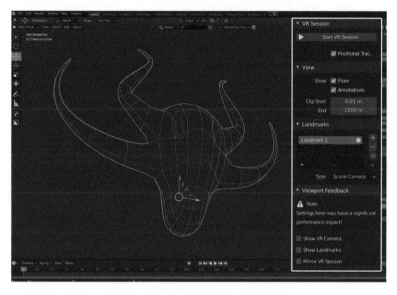

Figure 5-23. *Blender VR scene inspection settings*

Blender's plugin-enabled VR scene inspection is basic, but very often enough to evaluate a visual concept in VR, but to integrate interaction and locomotion, it is necessary to export the scene to Unity or Unreal.

5.4.3 The Mixed Reality Toolkit (MRTK)

Microsoft's Mixed Reality Toolkit (MRTK) is a cross-platform input system for UI and spatial interaction. The framework enables rapid prototyping with an extensive library of interaction modules. While most often used with HoloLens 2 projects, it also supports OpenXR, Windows Mixed Reality, and Oculus headsets, among others.

MRTK supports VR controllers, but is best used with direct hand interaction, where it shows its unique strength. Its interaction modules represent a state-of-the-art and robust, future-proof AR toolkit with support for both Unity (MRTK for Unity) and the Unreal engine (UXT, MRTK-Unreal, and UX Tools). Korean MRTK evangelist Dong Yoon Park has been sharing his developer insights over the years, including such specialized areas as typography for spatial computing as well as introducing typical use cases for MRTK UX building blocks.

The MRTK's distant object interactions are somewhat similar to the Oculus hand interaction concept, with a visible selection ray and air tab activation, in addition to unique MRTK gestures such as palm up to launch new content. Most of the basic interactions are consistent across all XR platforms, except where it is addressing specific HoloLens features, such as touch events with the HoloLens articulated hand or eye tracking and voice commands. The highlights of the MRTK are its well-thought-out, customizable interaction and UI modules. Next to basic interactions, as grabbing, rotating, and scaling objects, it provides a lineup of noteworthy modules for typical UX/UI problems (Figure 5-24).

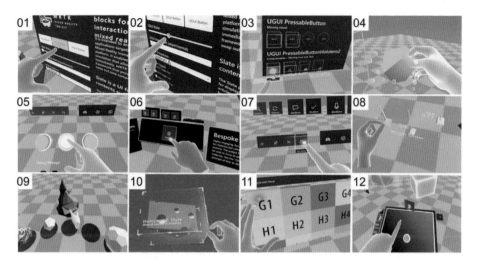

Figure 5-24. *Examples of MRTK interactions: (01) UI button interaction, (02) UI slider, (03) volumetric UI buttons, (04) snapping, (05) 3D buttons, (06) elastic interaction, (07) individual volumetric UI buttons, (08) 3D pinch slider, (09) docking, (10) bounding box manipulation, (11) pan and zoom gestures, (12) object color manipulator*

UI button interaction (01): The button behaves in a similar way as touch interaction for a mobile and web UI. On hover, the button highlights. On finger touch, or overlap, it changes color and activates.

UI slider (02): Behaves as a touch interface a user would expect. On hover, the button highlights. On finger touch, or overlap, it changes color and is draggable to the desired position.

Volumetric UI buttons (03): Buttons as part of a 2D menu that become 3D on approximation or are permanently visible as a 3D shape.

MRTK offers a variety of options, including the option to have the button's text and icon be pushed down with the mechanic or to have it in a fixed position on the UI. The button gives visual color change feedback on hover, press, and activation.

Snapping (04): Interval snapping to snap 3D objects into spatial positions. Typically used to guide the user into predefined interface slots, when moving UI elements and interaction components.

3D buttons (05): 3D buttons that look and behave like the real thing, plus the added event color changes, when the button is pushed down and triggered by the finger with an overlap event.

Elastic interaction (06): By adding a spring system, based on an elastic simulation, the MRTK enables engaging and fun UI events to swing open UI panels with bouncy animations. Adding these physics-based simulations brings delightful playfulness to the user's UI interaction.

Individual volumetric UI buttons (07): Other than the UI panel buttons, these buttons stand alone or are lined up in a button row. Typically, the 3D wireframe extension becomes visible on proximity and activates on finger touch/overlap with visual feedback through color changes.

3D pinch sliders (08): Like their counterparts in the real world, these sliders can be dragged into position. The finger pinch gesture acts as a trigger, next to touch/overlap, to simulate the haptics of a real slider.

Docking (09): Moveable 3D interaction and UI objects often have a home position. The docking feature indicates the default space of the object, where an object can be picked up and returned. Typically, docking resets its scaling, rotation, and scale value, when snapping back into the home position, overriding the manipulation values generated by the user.

Bounding box manipulation (10): Following the conventions of 3D desktop applications and games, bounding box manipulation handles allow the user to scale and rotate an object, depending on which part of the bounding box wireframe is activated. Options include having the bounding box visible at all times or activating it on proximity.

Pan and zoom gestures (11): Similar to touch interactions on mobile devices, the pan-zoom feature lets the user move the UI surface by pushing it with the interacting hand on touch/overlap. Moving both hands together or apart on the surface enables the user to zoom in or out of the UI content, if enabled.

Object color manipulator (12): Color customization is a popular feature in creative XR applications. The object color manipulator enables this feature with a pop-up customization panel to tweak color value setting by sliding the finger to the desired value coordinate, as it is typical for touch interaction on mobile devices.

The examples of typical MRTK interactions demonstrate the solid foundation for direct hand manipulation, addressing the most common UI and object interaction types for XR applications. The building blocks and elements range from traditional to playful and intuitive concepts that don't require tutorials or explanation, because the ideas are based on familiar concepts that users already understand. These familiar concepts are as follows:

- 2D web and mobile app touch interaction: For XR hand interaction, touch is replaced with overlap, while the base mechanics remain the same.

- 3D object interaction used in desktop applications and games: Move, rotate, and scale using bounding box object manipulation, common in 3D apps and games and which works the same way, by replacing mouse pointer or touch action with finger pinch in XR.

- Real-world physical interaction: Objects behave the same as their real-world counterpart. Buttons are pushed, sliders are moved, and objects are grabbed, pushed, and thrown according to their physical attributes. Real-world haptic resistance is replaced with overlap events and gestures, often supported with sound events for feedback.

The takeaway for UX design is that the majority of the MRTK interactions are addressing areas for the user that are intuitively understood, because they are based on familiar concepts and mental models.

VR applications often use an in-game tablet as a portable menu for the same reason: Users are familiar with mobile devices and feel comfortable using a familiar device as a central menu in VR.

The MRTK takes familiar concepts a step further and enhances UI conventions with 3D mechanics to add clarity, visual feedback, and playfulness to the interaction. A pressable 3D wireframe button as an extension of the 2D UI menu follows the expected mechanical behavior in its push-down mechanic, while the volumetric visual color change feedback makes it more satisfying to use. Bouncy UI panels with spring-powered physics behaviors add a level of playful fun when expanding a menu panel in a similar way. A fun interface keeps the user engaged.

As mentioned previously, the MRTK does not only support intuitive, direct hand interaction, but it also supports XR controllers, with typical controller button-activated direct interaction and selection ray distant interaction, enhanced by intuitive behavior when pulling objects in and manipulating 3D content.

The strength of the MRTK is the vast amount of modules, and the options to tweak module behaviors, next to cross-platform availability supported by the Unity and Unreal engines, in addition to an active developer community and a large amount of learning resources.

5.4.4 Prototyping an XR UI with Desktop UX/UI Tools

Prototyping menu interaction in XR by focusing only on the UI part of the application is a way to make sure the visual design system of the application, including the typography, colors, icons, and key visuals, is working as expected on a VR or AR device.

If the UI design is very sensitive and part of a larger brand architecture, where design system elements have to be consistent across various media channels, it is often necessary to verify that typography, color palette, iconography, and other UI design elements, including images, transfer well into XR.

Typical issues that may arise are these: hard to read text, flickering type, and UI items that may be difficult to see or understand due to viewing angle and viewing distance or device limitations. Light typeface legibility could suffer on curved screens, and small buttons or UI elements could make activation unnecessarily difficult. When designing a UI using a desktop tool, a quick menu check in XR can reveal the issues instantly and get the guesswork out of the way.

The plugin ecosystem of UX/UI applications Sketch, Figma, and Adobe XD, among others, is constantly coming up with new solutions, some of which survive only for a short time, as in the case for Torch AR, which supported an active Figma link. Currently, a plugin called DraftXR enables Adobe XR users to quickly preview a UI prototype in VR, by exporting it to a supported VR-compatible browser (Figure 5-25).

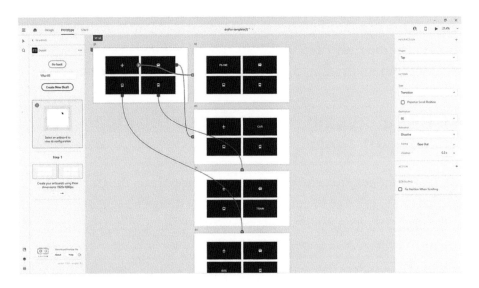

Figure 5-25. *The DraftXR plugin for Adobe XD*

DraftXR is a quick and easy way to preview an interface prototype with a headset, before building its final version using a game engine. It gives a quick first, albeit limited, XR preview of the UI, to evaluate typefaces, colors, and UI elements. Another option is to bring the design elements and Photoshop layers directly into the game engine for testing. A number of game engine plugins help with this process. The Unreal engine plugin *PSD2UMG*, for example, converts a PSD file into the Unreal engine UI widget format UMG (Figure 5-26).

Figure 5-26. *The PSD2UMG plugin in the Unreal marketplace*

In a similar way, the Unity plugins, *Psd 2 uGUI Pro* and *Psd Import*, allow developers to quickly import desktop UI concepts and test them with a VR test scene using Unity.

5.4.5 VR, AR, MR: The Evolution of Prototyping

The tools and the plugin ecosystem for creative XR prototyping have improved considerably over the last decade. Game engines and XR frameworks have become more user-friendly, with better learning resources and a growing plugin ecosystem, providing specialized solutions. The future of VR and AR applications, where these technologies are blended together in shared MR spaces, will require consistencies regarding interaction standards and UI conventions. Microsoft's MRTK is a preview of this world where the interaction concept scales across device categories and is shared between VR and AR in a multiuser MR environment.

5.5 VR Tours: 360 Video, VR180, and Immersive Photo Tours

One often overlooked area of immersive media is the 360/180 VR video and photo tour (VR tour) segment. Other than gaming, educational, and enterprise VR based on game engines, the VR tour segment uses 360 or VR180 video- and photo-capturing technology to deliver immersive media experiences based on camera-captured footage or images, delivered with hotspot activation, audio layers, and storytelling elements.

Immersive video/photo tours are more accessible to creators because, typically, no technical game engine knowledge is required and a variety of creation tools, which are more in line with cinematographic postproduction knowledge, give photographers, filmmakers, designers, and creators a way to build immersive experiences featuring existing locations.

VR tours have been commercially successful for real estate and hospitality communications, not just for VR headsets, but rather providing 360 views through a standard web browser. Users like to get an immersive view of a property or the vacation package, before committing to a purchase. The pandemic of 2020 made this use case even more compelling for situations where it was not possible to actually visit a location in person, due to public safety, travel, and meetup limitations. A wide range of 360/180 cameras are available and range from low-cost consumer to high-end broadcast devices.

There are five main formats to consider:

– 360 photos

– Stereoscopic 360 photos

– 360 videos

– Stereoscopic 360 videos

– Stereoscopic VR180 videos

The stereoscopic versions of a photo and a video require a different image for each eye, typically captured with a top-bottom or side-by-side arrangement. VR180 is a unique format, intended to deliver the best possible stereoscopic content quality in front of the viewer, as the pixel density and resolution is used for the front-facing space only, instead of distributing the resolution to 360 degrees, including unused back-facing areas. This format is best suited for performances, concerts, theater, or any stage presentation, where users are focused on the presentation in front of the camera, whereas the 360 formats are better suited for exploration-type experiences, such as exhibitions, museums, and location tours.

Publishing a VR tour or presentation is as straightforward as uploading it to a social platform, such as YouTube, or a specific 360 platform dedicated to immersive media. Oculus provides a media management tool, Oculus Media Studio, to support professional creators, with publishing and analyzing tools and a direct pipeline to Oculus TV, plus the additional out-of-headset discovery opportunities of its social networks (Figure 5-27).

Figure 5-27. *Oculus Media Studio*

5.5.1 VR Tour Content Creation and UX Considerations

The majority of VR tour creation tools are web based and are accessible through VR headset browsers using WebVR. Immersive web-based tools are often primarily intended to be used on desktop and mobile devices using a web browser. The available option to enter the space using a VR headset is typically an added bonus feature, while VR headset usage is growing toward mass adoption. The matterport.com toolset, for example, creates a 3D virtual web tour from 360 images that can be shared across social media, but it also supports VR walk-throughs, including free hotspot teleportation, using a headset like the Oculus Quest, when accessed through the Oculus web browser (Figure 5-28).

Figure 5-28. *A Matterport tour using the Oculus Quest*

VR tours or presentations that use linear video, instead of interactive photo tours using hotspots, have to consider that the UX begins on the film set. An immersed user requires onboarding with introduction footage, and the visual storytelling is ideally supported by balanced image composition using orientation anchors to make the user feel comfortable. The user takes the camera's point of view (POV) and becomes a character in the narrative, while the environment should spark their curiosity with points of interest and contextual information.

Special consideration of stabilized smooth transitions should be taken when a moving camera is used, as every unexpected movement is accelerated in VR, potentially disruptive and a cause for discomfort and nausea. In the case of stereoscopic media, the stereoscopic image composition becomes essential for a satisfying experience; typically includes a foreground, middle ground, and background; and should be consistent within an immersive sequence. Practices that are common with traditional media, such as video crossfades, often don't work with stereoscopic footage. Instead, a fade to black followed by a fade from black to open the next scene gives the user time to visually adjust.

Consistency is also required for eyeline matching. As the camera represents the user's POV and assumes a specific character height, it should be used consistently. Classic storytelling principles as guiding attention with imaginary continuity, visual tension and conflict, identification, and causality are as important as the fact that immersed users prefer shorter segments and rest periods, because of the higher intensity of the medium. The power of immersive storytelling is putting the user in the shoes of the narrator, thus creating empathy in a way not possible with other media types. The tools and techniques to enhance this experience play out to any content category, may it be an art exhibition or a first-hand report from a nature preservation project.

5.5.2 Adding Narrative Elements to VR Tour Media

One of the most flexible tools to build a VR tour using a mix of immersive media types is the application Pano2VR from Austrian developer Garden Gnome GmbH, next to the wide variety of applications between 3dvista.com and the video app building tool headjack.io. The Pano2VR desktop application is able to edit, patch, link, and map immersive photos and videos, enhanced by interactive elements, hotspots, and pop-ups, and overlay it with a narrative audio track, for immersive website experiences that are compatible with contemporary VR headsets (Figure 5-29).

Figure 5-29.   *The Pano2VR editor*

Pano2VR works with WebVR and can be shared from a web page or the third-party application VR Tourviewer, which is available on SideQuest. VR Tourviewer enables offline viewing and comes in different configurations, including a commercial white label solution with splash screen, menu, and UI customization options (Figure 5-30).

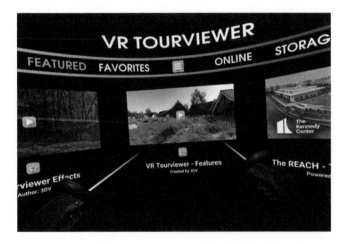

Figure 5-30.   *The free SideQuest version of VR Tourviewer*

Pano2VR plus VR Tourviewer provides a flexible solution to mix and match immersive media types, process the most popular formats, and design a guided tour setting with hotspot triggers and additional media layers. The solution is able to produce an intuitive and easy-to-use experience, with familiar point and click interaction, that even inexperienced users feel immediately familiar with.

The option to add background sound and audio narration, plus pop-up windows with additional information and image and video content, opens the door to a rich presentation in VR.

The user experience for VR tours is, for the most part, driven by the visual composition and the quality of its media sequences, as well as its narrative structure. Writing the script and scribbling the storyboard to map out the structure, in addition to an interaction flowchart, help to visualize the user flow and how it unfolds when activating a point of interest.

5.6 Summary

This chapter explored the pioneering platforms, tools, and media solutions to address XR experiences for handheld AR, Oculus headsets, HoloLens-based AR interactions, and solutions suited for immersive 360 media. Each of these examples represents an evolving segment of the industry with an active ecosystem of tools for designing, prototyping. and testing the next wave of media innovation. XR has been called the greatest revolution in the history of UX design for its narrative potential of space. To design this digital space efficiently, with compelling stories and meaningful experiences, one needs to understand the rulebook of this paradigm shift, its potential, and its underlying infrastructure, as it is evolving. UX XR designers are the architects of future realities, pioneering and mapping out the digital spaces that humans will inhabit once they are livable enough to stay.

CHAPTER 6

Practical Approaches: UX and XR in the Real World

6.1 Introduction

This chapter will examine the UX design process for an experimental XR product in development. How are the established UX methods playing out for a digital experience, bridging between two emerging technologies, XR and the blockchain? How practical are user empathy maps, and how to transition from the touch points of a user journey to a spatial experience? What tools or practices can be utilized to be more efficient, when transitioning from low-fidelity to high-fidelity prototype? XR gives designers more problems to solve, but it also opens doors to new methods in user research and data acquisition for testing, for example, when using WebVR-based user interaction. Along with exploring these new approaches, this chapter will wrap up with fundamental thoughts on where this era of the human-machine interface (HMI) will take us as a society, as individuals and, in particular, as designers, balancing powerful opportunities with new responsibilities.

© Cornel Hillmann 2021
C. Hillmann, *UX for XR*, https://doi.org/10.1007/978-1-4842-7020-2_6

Design thinking can help us to build better products, including better digital XR products. One way for the creative process to validate ideas before these are implemented in the real world is by asking the question: "What if…?" "What if we rethink our business and build a platform for a different type of user?" It is an opportunity to deep-dive into a new realm, to understand the context of it, what motivates users, and how it plays into a business strategy. Design thinking is about understanding where services or products could go, but from the user's perspective. It is a way to solve big product development questions and tackle the unknown.

The following case study starts with design thinking and a deep dive into the factors at play: It raises the question of how art collectors will use XR in the future. It is a scenario of how design thinking helps to take on fundamental questions, followed by the UX design process to get an understanding of the problems, opportunities, and solutions in the evolving XR space and its connected technologies.

This experimental and simplified case study goes through the steps from initial brief to testing, with the goal to illustrate the different steps in the process and how the problems are approached. It is an example of an ongoing project that will continue to be developed while reacting to changes in the business environment as part of its evolution.

6.2 Case Study: Gallery X, Part 1

The initial product idea for this case study was born out of hypothetical thinking: How will consumers shop for collectibles, home decoration, and art 20 years from now, in the year 2041? The design brief summary for the gallery (here called Gallery X) in 2021: "Gallery X is reaching out to VR users to establish new virtual exhibition formats to display pioneering digital art formats and genres, including NFT collectibles and crypto art."

The background: Gallery X has identified active VR users as a growing audience for digital art. There are currently 2 million VR users on Steam, with a growth rate of 94 percent year on year. Digital art, especially collectible NFTs (nonfungible tokens: unique blockchain tokens, functioning as an authenticity certificate), also labeled as "crypto art," is rapidly growing in popularity. VR exhibitions of crypto art have caught on with social VR spaces like VRChat and are part of the core idea behind dedicated VR blockchain spaces such as decentraland.org and cryptovoxels.com, among others. At the same time, there are also skeptical voices with concerns over excessive energy consumption, the overall carbon footprint of the crypto space, high network fees, as well as questions over extreme market volatility, monetary transparency, trust, and accountability (Figure 6-1). The research data reveal a division among VR gamers, among them a fraction showing skeptical to negative attitudes toward crypto-related topics, partially due to the fact that crypto mining has affected the availability and prices of high-end gaming graphic cards, often needed for PC VR, as crypto miners scoop up gaming hardware.

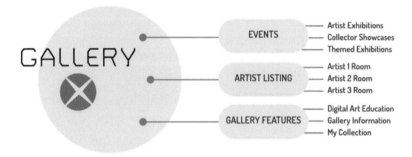

Figure 6-1. *Gallery X concept (image by C. Hillmann)*

The findings of research and user interviews were later utilized for an affinity map and ideation workshop, as the first step of the following UX workshops for this project.

6.2.1 Prototyping Utopia

VR galleries, digital art, NFT collectibles, and crypto art are a highly dynamic field that is rapidly evolving. It is partially a gold rush and potentially a bubble, plus a market that, as a result of the boom, is being flooded with new releases. Gallery X has identified this as an opportunity to create a destination for discovery and curation of digital art targeting crypto-friendly VR users. The goal is to have a foot in the door of this growing market segment, with the option to open up additional services in the future, whenever it becomes feasible.

During the deep dive, it helped to visualize the future 20 years from now, what role NFTs could have and how digital art could become part of an augmented environment, where virtual collectibles would exist in the contextual physical space. Visualizing the future VR NFT space helped to come up with scenarios, with the user as an NFT art collector expressing their personality through their collection, partially in their private space, in digital wall frames, private augmented spaces, as well as shared VR spaces online. The concerns of energy consumption being long resolved as leading blockchains have moved to the environmentally friendly Proof of Stake (PoS) concept.

It also helped to look 20 years back in history to explore the role of innovation mindsets and market forces. In 2001, there was the Dot-Com bubble, a time in history when excessive short-term expectations were crushed, but longer-term vision prevailed. Zapping from 2001 to 2021 and onward to 2041, future speculation helps to grasp the dynamic macro factors and forces at play. As early 2021 could turn out to be an NFT bubble, the substantial user benefit of the technology would most likely outlive market volatility. This research and discovery process helped to inspire ideation and identify pains and gains for the brand.

6.2.2 VR Gallery X: The Initial Design Brief

The initial design brief for the VR gallery covered the outline, scope, deliverables, timeline, and direction for the project, updated with changes as the project progressed. The following are the main points in the brief:

Primary objective:

Design a VR gallery for digital art. VR users should be able to discover, bookmark, and interact with digital art, including crypto art. The gallery is intended as a place of discovery and promotion for artists as well as collector exhibitions in an immersive gallery space with direct links to NFT marketplaces. Keywords: Discovery, context, curation.

Target audience and market:

The VR gallery is intended for active VR users. The primary audience is tech-savvy, crypto-friendly VR gamers, collectors, and investors, plus anyone with access to a VR headset and enthusiastic about digital art.

Project-specific information:

The gallery's goal is to curate digital art and provide a VR space to artists and collectors, providing valuable information and purchase recommendations. Artists, collectors, art promoters, and gallerists will be able to purchase promotional spaces and event slots. One of the core concepts is that artists and collectors are equally important. Space and importance are equally allocated to featured artists and featured collectors, providing a friendly, engaging, and immersive exhibition space.

Competitor information:

Digital art, crypto art, 3D and VR art, and NFT collectible destinations such as cryptovoxels.com, decentraland.org, and somniumspace.com, the Museum of Other Realities (museumor.com), ArtGateVR.com, and Museum of Contemporary Digital Art (mocda.org). Organizations and XR exhibition spaces that are part of the evolving and emerging digital art and NFT collectible space.

Deliverables:

A tested and working prototype, compatible with contemporary VR headsets.

6.2.3 VR Gallery X: Discovery

During the discovery phase of the project, qualitative data were gathered by facilitating stakeholder (interviews should be with at least six to eight individuals) and user interviews. Each of those user interviews followed the same script to find and compare possible patterns, behaviors, and expectations, confirming persona characteristics and addressing main insights. These insights can be summarized in the following way:

1. VR users who have a positive attitude toward a digital art VR gallery worry that there is not enough to do.

    Possible solution: Provide information in a more engaging way.

2. VR users sympathetic toward crypto art have concerns over the carbon footprint, networking ("gas") fees, as well as the trustworthiness of crypto platforms.

    Possible solution: Provide information on crypto quality of showcased art, including carbon footprint.

3. Research also showed that VR users would like to share their collections with their friends on social media.

    Solution: Provide a link to a companion web page with personal collections.

Overall, VR users would like to see interesting exhibition locations and interact with other users. Most desired features were an art wish list, a "Like" button for art, art sharing on social media, and a shareable private collection room.

VR users who were most interested in collecting digital art were also often interested in traditional collectibles such as trading cards, had an above-average disposable income, and were actively trading using investment apps such as Robinhood. During user interviews, questions over legitimacy of the nonfungible token (NFT) concept became apparent, as well as how the integrity of the link between digital art file and the blockchain data unit is guaranteed. It became apparent that an optional introduction to blockchain technology and the NFT concept would add value as a gallery resource for new users. This educational introduction would explain the role of traditional art certificates in contemporary art and how this established concept can transfer into the digital realm. During stakeholder interviews, it became clear that the goal was to curate art and become a premium destination for discovery of digital art, with the option to add additional services at later stages. Stakeholders saw an opportunity to build a mixed-media platform, bringing together different formats, including non-NFT collectibles, and to create value with contextual information that is often lacking with established marketplaces. Featuring artists and collectors and their stories, as well as themed exhibitions based on location, subject, and cause, would allow Gallery X to grow with advertising and bookable XR space. In summary:

Challenge statement:

VR users were unsure about the idea of NFTs, but liked the idea to share personal collections of digital art.

Solution statement:

To create a VR experience that introduces digital art and personal collection spaces and to provide digital art information, including NFT background information.

6.2.4 VR Gallery X: Exploration

To gain more insights regarding the digital arts field, a competitive analysis alongside market research and a user empathy map with a main persona was created.

The competitive analysis revealed that most digital art destinations were primarily focused on crypto investors and gamers and featured basic game graphics and no collector showcases or advanced social features. At the same time, non-crypto-art VR galleries focused on digital art did not provide a pathway to collecting and to shareable art ownership with social features, but they provided better-looking environments (Figure 6-2).

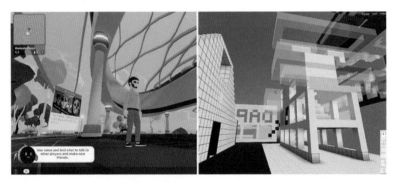

Figure 6-2. *NFT market research: decentraland.org and cryptovoxels.com*

All research was brought together in a synthesis to get a fundamental understanding of the products and the user. The empathy map based on qualitative user interviews revealed a number of problems and challenges. The map was visualized with four quadrants: Says, Thinks, Does, and Feels (see Figure 4-2 in Chapter 4).

Says describes what the user was actually saying. Thinks means to assess the thinking behind the user's actions. Does describes the actual behavior of the user. Feels describes the actual emotions and feelings of the user. The resulting board sections helped to understand the persona and its pain points:

Says:

How can I download or save images?

I want to build my collection.

How can I share my collection on social media?

I only invest into things I believe in.

Which featured artist has the most potential?

It's hard to decide what to pick.

Thinks:

I hope I remember the controller button settings.

I am confused about the different options.

I hope I am lucky to pick the right thing.

I'm excited to discover new things.

I'm entertained by the exhibits.

I wonder what carbon footprint this crypto art piece has.

Does:

Researches on websites for trending collectibles.

Compares products.

Subscribes to investment newsletters.

Asks family, friends, and colleagues for their opinions.

Teaches others what they have learned.

Ends applications if irritated or bored.

Feels:

Unsure about selections.

Excited to find something new.

Fear of not using the application correctly.

Overwhelmed with options.

Bored with limited selection.

6.2.5 Persona, User Journey, and User Story

The next step in this process was to move from the empathy map describing a persona group to a specific persona. In this example: Todd, a 35-year-old insurance broker. The persona card describes his profile, including (a) Needs, wants & expectations, (b) Motivations & attitudes, (c) Frustrations, (d) Bio, (e) Goals, and (f) Channel or product preferences (Figure 6-3).

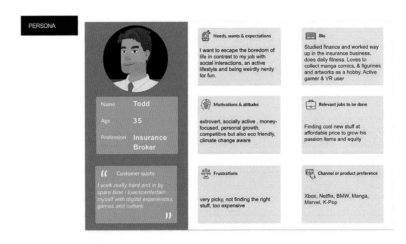

Figure 6-3. *Persona: Todd (Photo replaced with cartoon image for privacy reasons)*

Using the persona, a user journey was mapped out (Figure 6-4). The user journey map was divided into the first three sections of the experience.

Onboarding:

An introduction about the gallery, setting expectations and with instructions for the controller button functions

Lobby:

A space where the user decides which exhibition or feature to use

Exhibition room:

An artist exhibition, or theme exhibition, art event, or collector's showcase

The important part was to show what the user's thoughts at each of the experiences, actions, and touch points were and what opportunities these would reveal. Examples:

Phase of journey: Onboarding.

Action: Looking at screen with controller button functionality.

Touch point: Instruction screen.

User thought: I hope I remember this.

Opportunities: Include help button, always accessible.

Phase of journey: Lobby.

Action: Looking at different environment objects and features .

Touch point: Interactive object.

User thought: I'm confused. Hopefully, I decide on a good one (I don't want to waste my time).

Opportunities: Show popular events, star ratings, or likes.

Phase of journey: Artist's exhibition room.

Action: Interacts with artwork.

Touch point: Info/activate.

User thought: I wonder what the carbon footprint for this crypto art piece is.

Opportunities: Show carbon footprint info for each art piece.

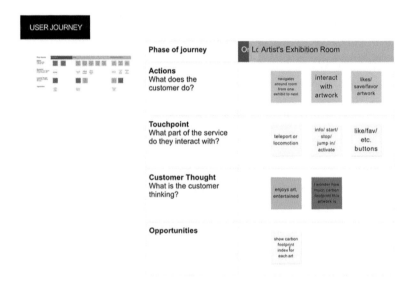

Figure 6-4. *The artist exhibition room section of the user journey*

Persona and user journey were used to create a user story (Figure 6-5).

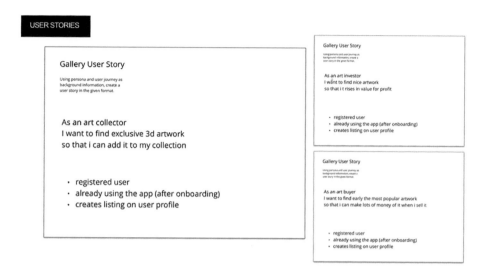

Figure 6-5. *The user story*

6.2.6 Object-Oriented UX in an XR Context

The next step of the process was to identify the object the user interacts with and define their functions and relationships. This part refers to the Object-Oriented UX (OOUX) methodology described in Chapter 4. OOUX with an XR context is used with slightly different priorities and objectives compared to its typical application. While it can target any media format due to its platform agnostic nature, it is also an intuitive way to directly discover what actual XR scene objects appear in the spatial journey and how these objects will recur in varying relationships and functions during the different sections of the experience. The object discovery in the first part (object definition) followed by object functions (create object functions) is driven directly by the user journey. The objects are extracted from the user journey map and its functions and touch points identified on the first OOUX board (Figure 6-6). For example:

Object definition: Onboarding stage

Touch point reference: Onboarding screen

Object: Controller function

Create object functions for: Onboarding

Defined object (from previous board): Controller function

Object functions: Control button explanation, visual guides, menu location

CTA: Next, Skip all

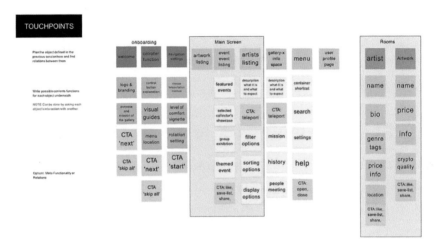

Figure 6-6. *Object touch points*

The next OOUX board is dedicated to the object relationships of its main objects. The object name is followed by its attribute, its function, and its nested objects. Nested objects are listed at the bottom of each individual object to visualize the relationship (Figure 6-7). For example:

Object: Artwork

It is part of this listing: Artwork listing
(on top of row)

Object attribute: Title

Object function: Select

Nested objects: Artist, Visitor, Event

The nested objects reveal how the *Artwork* object depends on other objects.

Nested object *Artist*: An *Artwork* reveals the information about the *Artist*.

Nested object *Visitor*: A *Visitor* shortlists, shares, or buys an *Artwork*.

Nested object *Event*: An *Artwork* is part of an *Event* (like an exhibition).

After defining the object relationships, they will be added to the touchpoints. Prioritizing and force-ranking objects becomes important, especially if the objects and features are high in numbers and the goal is to build an MVP prototype.

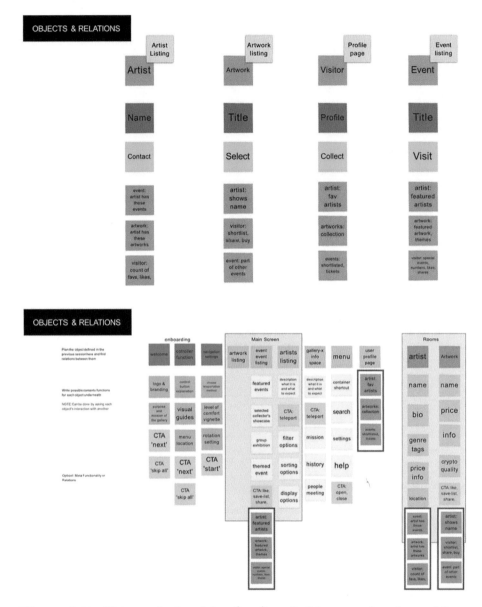

Figure 6-7. *Object relationships (top) and object touchpoints with added object relationships (bottom)*

At this point, we are establishing a good idea of the objects in the VR experience. The object-oriented approach helps to identify how the user interacts with XR objects while at the same time helping to establish an information architecture applicable to the spatial experience. In the next steps of this process, we will turn to the prototyping stage, creating storyboards followed by mapping storyboard objects to XR framework features.

6.3 Case Study: Gallery X, Part 2, Thinking, Designing, Building, Testing

The first version of the storyboard is a verbal description based on the user story, written out in stages through a sequence of actions on a timeline.

6.3.1 The Verbal Storyboard

The verbal storyboard contains six scripted steps and is user story based.

Onboarding (1):

Gallery X logo with audio branding and loading animation.

Onboarding (2):

Display help screen with controller button instruction: "Skip" or "Next" button.

Lobby (3):

Three scene objects that display information. Object 1—: Screen with exhibition events. Object 2—: Screen with artist listings. Object 3: Screen with gallery features. Interaction with the event screen.

Artist exhibition (4):

A gallery room with a lineup of framed NFT artworks on the wall.

Artwork interaction (5):

Showing teleportation interaction.

Artwork interaction (6):

Interaction with the info symbol next to the artwork.

The info display panel shows a description of the artwork: a short profile of the artist, with an "Info" button and an artist and artwork information detail page and a "Stats" button with a crypto quality information detail page. The dashboard bottom has three buttons to activate: (a) Like, (b) Wish list, (c) Share.

6.3.2 The Visual Storyboard and Low-Fidelity Prototype

The visual storyboard and user flow takes the written stages and conceptualizes the visual features by sketching with pen and paper, followed by 3D mockups using Blender 3D and Gravity Sketch in VR. Sketching helps to rough out a 3D layout, get quick feedback, do impression testing, and come up with the visual concept and basic ideas through ideation (Figure 6-8).

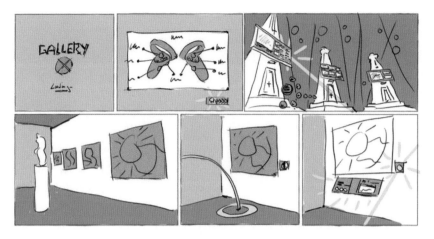

Figure 6-8. *Storyboard sketches (image by C. Hillmann)*

The sketched storyboard provides the template to rough out a spatial layout in 3D by grayboxing with Blender and Gravity Sketch. When modeling out environment ideas in Blender, it is a good idea to use real-world scale so that the scene's real-world dimensions transfer correctly to VR. Using Blender, or any other DCC application with a 3D modeler, is an efficient way to assemble the most important assets for an early visualization, from early grayboxing to more detailed concepts at a later stage. Developing visual ideas, a color palette, iconography, and the overall visual design system was done in the later process, while the spatial layout was evaluated. Visual language, including typography, key images, and brand ID, was conceptualized using mood boards. The goal was to evaluate the visual design ideas during the prototyping stage, to iterate and to prioritize the ideas that worked best in the 3D context (Figure 6-9).

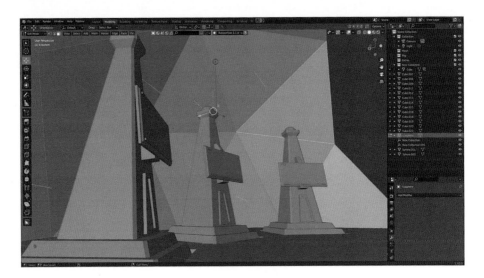

Figure 6-9. *Early grayboxing in Blender*

Importing a rough 3D layout into Gravity Sketch for modeling and layout tweaks helped to test the element in VR and get an idea of how it would feel, using a VR headset (Figure 6-10).

Figure 6-10. *Tweaking a scene in Gravity Sketch*

After adding more detail, it was important to get user and stakeholder feedback. Impression testing using methods like the popular five-second test allows for obtaining quick feedback to find out if the concept is working as intended. That is, let a user or stakeholder view the scene layout with a VR headset, possibly even without controllers, for only five seconds. This short amount of time is enough to get a first impression and assess if the design is able to communicate the intention as intended. To make impression testing effective and evaluate early feedback, a list of questions should be asked. The following are examples of VR impression testing questions:

> What elements do you remember from the scene?

> What subject matter is the VR scene about?

> What would you do next in this environment?

> Did the environment feel comfortable?

At this point, unclear scene elements, or irritating, distracting objects, can be rearranged, redesigned, or removed. Obtaining early feedback to evaluate and iterate design concepts is a way of getting on the right track upstream, instead of carrying a questionable idea into the prototyping stage without having it evaluated by users and stakeholders. It is a way to avoid unnecessary and extra work.

Once ideas, design concepts, and visual language have been narrowed down and the sketched storyboard is transitioned into a 3D low-fidelity ideation prototype, including all storytelling elements, it is time to identify XR framework functions and pin them to the visual concept as interactive elements.

This approach is part of a concept explained in Chapter 4 in the section "Case Study: Reality UX." Identifying framework functions at the early storyboard or ideation prototype stage helps to understand where existing components can make the prototyping process faster and easier. There is no reason to reinvent the wheel for every standard feature that is considered base functionality in a VR app, such as locomotion and teleportation. Being able to assess which features will fit the bill and which ones will need to be custom built is also an early assessment of the development scope.

The concept of Reality UX as a database for the majority of frameworks, including a reference system of identifying its comparable features, is a way of taking this idea one step further and to find the right framework match and engine platform for the right project.

For the VR Gallery X project, it was decided to use the Advanced Framework (AF) by humancodeable.org for the Unreal engine. The framework provides a number of customizable building blocks, including UI panels and radial menus, which were considered important for the project. By tagging the respective functions with unique IDs, providing a summary of the functionality, plus a link to further information, the Reality UX references put everyone in the team on the same page regarding how the interactions are expected to play out.

6.3.3 Building the High-Fidelity Prototype and Testing It

Having iterated design ideas, tested them with impression testing, and prioritized concepts that would be most important for a functional interactive prototype laid the groundwork for the actual interactive prototype production with the most important features. In this case, key features are the menu-activated user rooms, wish lists, shareable artwork, and the individual artwork info panel (Figure 6-11).

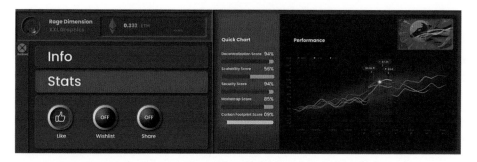

Figure 6-11. *Artwork dashboard info panel UI concept (image by C. Hillmann based on Figma Theme by @josh_abolade and @zazulyazizAziz)*

Because framework functions were tagged early on, identifying features in the storyboard using the Reality UX toolkit, in this case the Advanced Framework by humancodable.org, made it clear which functions needed to be activated. In our case, for example, it was the radial menu functions and the panel functions (Figure 6-12).

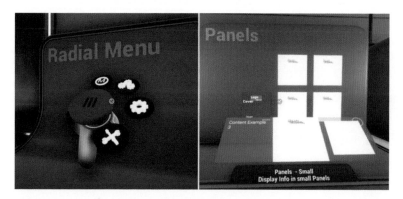

Figure 6-12. *Radial menu and panel functions from the Advanced Framework (humancodeable.org)*

Compared to web and mobile app prototyping, this stage is more time consuming and more complex, because 3D asset creation, including 3D modeling, texturing for PBR shading, and animations have to be considered, if applicable. Depending on the scope of the production, the 3D art pipeline takes considerably more time than the first phase of the project. Once 3D assets are designed, modeled, textured, and animated, they have to be assembled and staged in the game engine. Framework functions need to be adjusted, customized, and optimized in the context of the scene, and interactions need to be playtested to confirm that they work as envisioned. A high-fidelity prototype for a VR experience is typically very close to the final product in terms of visual fidelity and interactions, but most typically focuses on the core concept and the ideas that need to be evaluated with user testing (Figure 6-13).

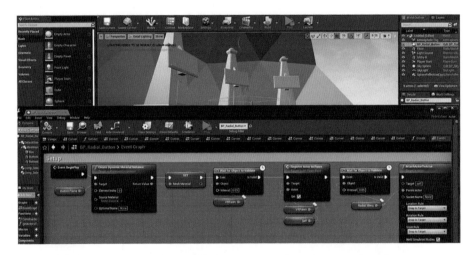

Figure 6-13. *Building a prototype with the Unreal engine*

Once the prototype becomes available for testing, decisions have to be made about how and where the testing will take place. If it is intended for the public, the SideQuest platform or Oculus App Lab can be considered, or an early access release on Steam. Public testing typically gets user reaction and, if encouraged, reports on usability and core concepts.

Most of the time, prototypes are not public, especially enterprise and B2B apps intended for a specialized audience and industry. In those cases, it is the best idea to send out the Android Package (APK) file, to be installed on targeted headsets of testing partners, or to do in-house testing using a headset that has the software installed via sideloading. The latter is the most common practice for small to medium projects, especially in the event and B2B space.

Once the APK file is installed via sideloading, users are invited to participate in the testing sessions. There are of course many different methods to test. For a VR application, it is most practical to monitor and record the user-testing session with a second screen and record it on the device or via the Oculus developer hub. The goal is to capture the users' interactions and comments and to get valuable insights on the most important features and identify pain points. Typically, these include user feedback for interactions where expectations are misaligned, actions are not completed, or features are not used. Testing in VR is a bit of a different ballgame than for other media, because usability is often the biggest talking point. Usability is one of the biggest concerns in XR, but it also tends to overshadow the more nuanced goals of the product. Almost everyone has a preference for such basic VR functions as locomotion and object interaction, and users can easily be irritated or distracted if these basics are used in a different way or need time to be customized or adjusted.

In principle, testing procedures follow the established standards with any digital product: starting the session with pre-testing questions, followed by giving the user tasks (instead of questions that can be answered with yes or no) and observing the user on the mirrored screen. In the case of the VR Gallery, the tasks are as follows:

> Let's go to the main menu.
>
> Move to another room.
>
> Find the event X.

Find your favorite style of artwork.

Or responding to specific actions of the user:

I noticed you never looked at the wish list room.
Why?

During the post-test, additional user questions were asked about the overall experience and the impressions of the project, such as:

What would you change?

How would you compare it to your favorite VR app?

What was the best thing about the experience? What was the worst?

All completed user tests were finally formatted into standard categories and tags employed in UX user testing, which therefore allowed us to draw conclusions from the data.

The user research helped to validate the prototype and detect a few usability issues; plus it helped to get insights on features that needed to be improved or gave inspiration for features that needed to be added.

Tweaks and iterations are fairly easy to do when using a framework that is already set up. This way, even small iterations and usability tweaks can be quickly implemented. The objective is to obtain unbiased data by testing, followed by tweaking features and iterating the prototype until things are right.

6.3.4 The Double Diamond Process and Its Results

The complete UX design process for the VR Gallery X project is reflected during the stages it passed through the double diamond (as shown in Chapter 4): diverging with user research, converging by narrowing down the main problems to solve, discovering objects in the user journey, mapping these objects and their relationships, then developing a storyboard from these objects and mapping them to XR framework features, and, at the next stage, building the high-fidelity prototype to test and iterate (Figure 6-14).

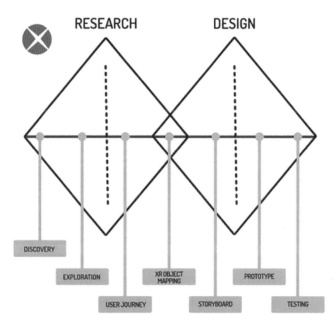

Figure 6-14. The double diamond timeline progression of VR Gallery X, referring to the stages discussed in this chapter (image by C. Hillmann)

The double diamond reflects the product development process, from idea to realization, passing through the user-centric evaluation phases. In the case of the VR Gallery X project, it brought a catalog of valuable insights to improve the product. For example, it became clear that more information resources regarding the concept of NFTs needed to be provided. Users felt insecure about the value and long-term investment outlook of NFTs. While no one can claim to know for sure, if the technology will have a prosperous future as crypto art enthusiasts and blockchain optimists propose, there is a good amount of contextual information and art trading context to explain.

VR is a great medium for educational purposes, as the immersive nature offers an interactive and audio-visual deep dive into complex subjects that are otherwise uninspiring to explain with web pages or videos. Immersive storytelling and data visualization for a subject that demonstrates the synergies and exciting potential of two emerging technologies, XR and the blockchain, are a tremendous opportunity. In this case, it opened up the prospect to explain the traditional role of the certificate for fine-art collectors and art dealers. The comparison becomes clear when considering certificates for contemporary art that is often not a physical object and, for example, can entail performance art. In these cases, the collector buys a certificate that documents their ownership, but more so, they become part of the artist's journey. This journey is more than owning a piece of property; it means to be part of a story, that is, ideally a growth story, as the artist gains recognition and becomes more valuable. Artists and collectors are equally important in this ecosystem, where cooperation, trust, and accountability play an important role. Throughout history, this system has been played behind closed doors in the ivory towers of the elitist fine-art collector world. NFTs are bringing this concept to the masses and ushering in a new creator economy that is essentially important for the emerging XR universe. Once the dust of hype and hysteria settles and blockchain-related issues are resolved, we will most likely see a new flourishing and accessible trading landscape. Once the domain of an exclusive elite, symbolized by such collector archetypes as J. Paul Getty, whose famous museum was an expression of his passion and personality, this ancient success formula of philanthropy and investment is unfolding in a democratized and accessible way for the digital economy. The emerging XR economy enables everyone to have a VR museum with their very own collection, not only as a shareable expression of personality but also as a way to show support for digital artists. And, last but not least, to see their commitment grow in value. The often-quoted main feature of NFTs, giving a collector "digital bragging rights," means nothing less than expressing personality by sharing a collector's journey in public. The vision behind the VR Gallery X project was to make this experience fun, engaging, and future-proof and empower it with the synergies of the emerging XR space and the potential of the blockchain-driven decentralized Web 3.0. The UX design process helped to identify the problems, narrow them down to the most important ones, build a solution with a prototype, and test it to iterate with changes and adjustments. The Reality UX toolkit (as described in Chapter 4) was used to first identify objects using the OOUX method, then define their attributes and relationships, and finally map them to VR framework functions using the storyboard.

One of the marketing philosophies and guiding principles to develop the VR Gallery X was the StoryBrand Framework, a storytelling formula to communicate the most important business messages to the user. Its mission is to make the user a hero of the brand and its story. Creator Donald Miller believed that brands solve the users' problem by being a guide. Brand storytelling is one of the major opportunities of immersive media in the experience economy. To tell a brand's story in XR means to go beyond the confines of 2D media formats and create a closer, more personalized connection with the user.

6.4 UX Strategy, Analytics, Data Acquisition, and UX Audits for XR Projects

Data acquisition by recording and tracking user behavior, in addition to user interviews, followed by its synthesis to gain insights from the data, is part of the UX research observation techniques. In principle, there is not much difference from web and mobile user research for acquiring data from XR users. XR will eventually have better tools for precision tracking of the user's motion, including eye movement, once the capture technology and its tools mature. Eye tracking, full-body tracking and recording, and even brain-computer interfaces (BCIs) are available on high-end systems or research projects, but it will take some time before these features bring their full potential to UX researchers, using analytics software tools and procedures in compliance with ethical standards and frameworks. In the meantime, the focus is on traditional user research, where it is sometimes difficult to get nuanced opinions in the face of the fact that XR experiences are still considered a novelty for casual users. The other problem is that XR user testing case studies and resources are sparse, except for the well-documented efforts of organizations willing to pioneer this field.

6.4.1 Mozilla XR Resources

One resource that stands out in the XR landscape are the online reports, tools, insights, and background information provided by the nonprofit organization Mozilla Foundation, known by most people for its open source software tools, including Firefox and Thunderbird. Since its founding in 1998, Mozilla has shaped the Internet as a counterbalance to corporations, with its mission statement to *put people over profit and advance the open, global Internet,* including the new frontiers of XR. Next to XR projects such as the Firefox Reality browser, WebVR, and A-Frame is Mozilla Hubs, a multiuser VR environment with customization options, including the 3D space creation tool Spoke. Mozilla regularly shares insights from its user research on blog.mozvr.com, thus providing resources that are often hard to come by, especially when observing methods for VR user research. The reports from Mozilla Hubs show, for example, that qualitative research with six tech-savvy users and their partners allowed the researcher to observe authentic interactions between participants for feedback, particularly for social VR products, in this case. One interesting insight was that the more the product was developed, the less technologically sophisticated the users needed to be. This finding confirms the notion that a low-fidelity prototype should ideally be reviewed by tech-savvy XR users with the ability to judge it based on its potential. In reverse, this means that it is often less useful to test a rough concept with users new to XR, even if they represent the target audience. To get the best results, including valuable direct user quotes, it is important to conduct pre-test and post-test interviews and to allow extra time for these users to get comfortable with controllers and navigation.

6.4.2 User Feedback Based on WebVR

WebVR is a very effective way to obtain user feedback on early ideas and concepts, especially for remote teams and in cases where it is difficult to meet up, as it has been during the Covid-19 pandemic. Mozilla is leading the way into the WebVR era, with a Unity web exporter package and its own multiuser WebVR space Mozilla Hubs (hubs.mozilla.com). The device-independent nature of WebVR makes any published link immediately accessible for remote testing. In the case of social VR spaces, using Hubs, for example, allows the tester to be there with the user, to observe and guide the process: an almost-ideal situation that is almost impossible to reach otherwise without a lengthy development process. WebVR empowers quick sharing, testing, and iterating, using a WebVR framework such as Mozilla's own A-Frame or a 3D creation tool such as Mozilla's Spoke (hubs.mozilla.com/spoke). With Spoke, it is possible to build a complete 3D scene using important assets and convert it into a social VR space for sharing and testing on Hubs (Figure 6-15).

Figure 6-15. *Mozilla Spoke (left) and Hubs (right)*

Spoke allows designers to validate a visual VR idea or spatial layout with basic layout playability testing by sharing a WebVR link. Very often, ideas have to be viewed in VR using a headset to see if the concept works or not. VR walk-throughs, including distances, heights, obstacles, room perception, and orientation, are dramatically different, compared to reviewing a 3D scene on a 2D screen. To test how users behave in a user research project is as straightforward as strolling through the environment with the user. Walking with the user through a VR environment gives the tester a chance to observe and ask questions regarding the environment layout, its object, and visual language. The process of recording this conversation can reveal user impressions regarding discoverability, guidance, navigation, possible confusion, unnecessary obstacles, and aesthetic confusion or appeal of its composition and visual appearance.

The approach of WebVR impression testing is obviously only suitable for early environment design tests and because of the limitation of WebVR and its interaction options. Overall, it is more suitable for a simple, stylized environment, as typically and often used in XR educational and training products.

An alternative to WebVR, Mozilla Hubs, and Spoke is to build a custom environment for Altspace. This approach currently requires to enable the Altspace World Beta features and the Altspace Unity plugin for uploading custom environments.

The advantage of a custom Altspace environment is to actually attract random walk-ins from Altspace users and recruit Altspace users currently on the platform or the opportunity to organize events in Altspace for user feedback. Altspace has been one of the longest-running social VR spaces, and its user base is typically mature, professional, and cooperative. That means an ideal situation in which to obtain feedback from a user base that has often strong VR affinity and valuable insights on VR content and its users. Altspace customization options are limited, but are expected to grow, considering the ambitious road map and vision for the Microsoft Mesh platform.

6.4.3 UX Audits for XR Projects

UX audits have been a successful concept in the digital economy, very often done to improve the performance of an ecommerce product. Typically, the goal is to eliminate UX issues and bring the customer experience in tune with business goals by providing data and actionable recommendations to solve the problems. In this way, the UX audit is like a UX design process, without the actual design execution. Instead, its final step is the assessment of the UX situation with findings and recommendations. Its process is to understand the users and their objectives, through user interviews and insights from acquired data, such as quantitative information based on user statistics, online reviews, and social media numbers. The other important part is to understand the business objectives, by acquiring the information through stakeholder interviews.

UX audits for XR products will become more important as the industry matures and ecommerce transactions become a regular part of AR and VR applications to purchase products and services. This development is foreshadowed by in-game purchases, add-ons, and unlockable content for current-generation XR games. Next to the typical ecommerce focus, there is also the usability review and the UX audit on other product KPIs, for example, replayability, user engagement, time spent, and user acquisition growth, typically measured by acquired usage data and assessing user behaviors and attitudes. Examples of relevant behavioral XR KPIs could be as follows:

> Abandonment rate: Frequency of an experience being ended before completion

> Conversions: Percentage of initial user registration in XR

> Problems and frustrations: Measurable usability issues, such as the number of menu steps to change interaction options

> Task success: Percentage of completed tasks from start to finish

> Task time: How long did it take to complete the task

> Attitudes that can be measured by a satisfaction score: The overall satisfaction and/or broken down into subcategories according to content and features

> Recommendation/social media score: Frequency of recommendations or shares on social media

6.5 Summary

This chapter demonstrated how UX design methods apply to spatial computing and how to approach the possible roadblocks of XR prototyping to avoid unnecessary inefficiencies by following a product development cycle through the UX lens. By going through research and discovery, defining persona and user journey, using object-oriented methods to map the XR space, the course of this chapter was able to ideate solutions, to build, test, and iterate an NFT art experience in a collaborative remote workshop–driven process. This experimental case study was able to validate UX principles in the XR space and explore its stages using the double diamond model. While discussing UX audit approaches and data acquisition, the chapter investigated the opportunities of social WebVR for early ideation and user testing. In the following conclusion, it will take a step back to look at the bigger picture of how the spatial narrative in immersive 3D spaces is unfolding and what it could mean for future societies and their designers as user advocates, when embarking on the XR journey into an unknown future of multilayered realities.

6.6 Conclusion: The Future Is Here

XR has arrived, it is being used by millions, yet it lives in a shielded niche, defined by Oculus with 53 percent of the wearable XR market, as VR headsets dominate with more than 90 percent of all XR headsets (according to Counterpoint Research, March 2021). XR is predominantly used for gaming, but rapidly growing in other areas such as enterprise, education, training, and social interaction. The XR industry is expected to scale up in double digits, once Apple enters with its own line of XR products. Companies like Microsoft are building an infrastructure for the next economy, and affordable AR wearables are expected to enter the mass market shortly. What we are witnessing is the biggest growth opportunity in the history of design (Figure 6-16). It took a good amount of time from Pong to Alyx, but things are moving faster this time.

Figure 6-16. *XR: The future of design (image by C. Hillmann)*

6.6.1 The Next Growth Story: UX for XR

As we enter the XR era, we still have a lot of questions awaiting answers. How can we optimize the patterns for XR interactions in a three-dimensional world that can be navigated? How do we organize complex information in a future-proof XR-compatible information architecture? Spatial mapping and providing users with instinctual interactions through body, hand, eye, and voice input is becoming part of the shared design journey. Surprisingly simple and obvious ideas, like the fist-bump gesture in Population: ONE to add a friend to one's friends list, are needed to make this new era engaging, delightful, and intuitive while using existing knowledge of the physical space to keep it comfortable. XR brings us into a design territory where atmospheric perspective creates a sense of depth and dimensionality. Our toolbox for this space contains motion parallax, relative size, shading, texture, perspective, and occlusion, while binaural audio helps us to map audio perception. At the same time, we need to build for different user types and allow customization for different heights, body types, abilities, fears, preferences, and comfort levels. Inclusive design, addressing users with different mental models, is just as important as positioning the UI at the right viewing area distance while providing consistency and feedback. UX designers have a lot on their plate as we transition into uncharted territory as pioneers and adventurers.

6.6.2 The XR Future: A Balance of Opportunities and Risk Mitigation

We are at the brink of a historic new era. Ten or twenty years from now, we'll look back at the early 2020s, puzzled by how smoothly the world shifted into the spatial computing era. By that time, we will live among XR natives, a generation that grew up with VR and AR, for whom it is the most natural thing to explore a new fitness device with an AR manual, to touch base with their friends' avatars while working in a virtual team office, before attending an afterwork, VR meetup to discuss virtual real estate investments. *XR-first* products will be standard and UX designers will help to make good things happen: designing meaningful XR products while maintaining user agency for some of the bigger concerns such as supporting appropriate governance mechanisms, including frameworks for data ownership, usage, consent, and protection. Personal data enter a new era, where biometric data, eye movement patterns, motion profiles, physical likeness, private environments, behaviors, and judgments as part of spatial user data will become increasingly available and potentially vulnerable to manipulation. VR pioneer Jaron Lanier pointed out that VR can become a beautiful bridge between people and the self as an expressive medium, but is symmetrically matched with the potential for real evil as the ultimate behavioral toolbox, if not governed properly, including the critical assessments of digital ownership.

There are reasons enough to be optimistic about a human-centered future of society fueled by the XR-driven imagination economy.

The next level of digital transformation has the potential to transition into a more ecological, greener economy. Digital is not green by default; it is to some degree plagued by high-energy consumption, e-waste, and digital pollution as a result of its legacy infrastructure, but it has the potential to unlock radical new levels of optimization for the organizational performance of a greener, more sustainable future.

The Covid-19 pandemic has shown us that corporate travel can be minimized without impacting a business, by pivoting to using virtual meetings. Virtual tourism is on its way to reducing the carbon footprint of bucket-list travel. A snippet from an overheard conversation demonstrates this notion: "I've seen the pyramids of Giza in VR; it was amazing, actually amazing enough to take it off my bucket list." How about fast retail? Humans love to shop: In comes the new, and out goes the old, including home decorations, furniture, and accessories. As global supply chains are choking the planet, we might ask: How about shifting the human compulsive shopping behavior to digital goods? A place where no tree gets hurt and no ships or containers need to be moved. Early promising concepts show how light, always-on, super high-resolution XR wearables could help to reskin the personal environment. Instead of buying a new dresser, keep the old one, but purchase a digital AR skin for it.

The digital goods economy has been very successful in the gaming world, where gamers reskin their avatars and purchase virtual accessories with microtransactions. This model is just waiting to spill into the real world, once we are mapping and remapping our environments and pining virtual objects over physical items. An information layer can be much more than just functional; it can be profoundly aesthetic. "You thought you could never reside in a nineteenth-century chateau with a park view. Just wait until you're able to remap your apartment accordingly" could be the tagline for a remapped XR future. At the same time, this could mean that we eliminate the unpleasant while designing our own reality bubble, on a level never experienced before. But with opportunities comes serious responsibility. How will we be dealing with remapping humans? This question will bring the deep-fake debate to a whole new level. Designing our own reality has an incredible potential. Responsible UX design will play an important part in the process of finding the balance between opportunities and mitigating risks.

6.6.3 XR Futurism: Designing Reality

The immersive tech revolution is just catching up with science fiction. We will be waking up to a new world that is enhancing our natural senses and collective imagination by blurring physical and virtual boundaries. As we shift into the imagination economy, we are shifting from the viewer to the participatory paradigm, where the 3D space is the narrative potential and the palette. It is a new rulebook that designers have to conquer, learn, and refine. The UX job market will be on fire, beyond anything we have seen yet, once the XR revolution unfolds. Every industry and business will need an XR approach. Considering the fact that the term *experience* in UX was more aspirational than literal when originally introduced, it now seems an almost prophetic manifestation for the true destination of designers, to design an immersive spatial dimension that previously never existed in UX, where physical movement, distance, and body, hand, and head movement are essential parts of the interaction. The emerging language of usability systems and data architecture using the XR canvas and its narrative aspects of spatial information will empower the user, who will, in turn, be able to design their own perception. As human consciousness is a product of perception, this ultimately means we are reinventing ourselves as a species. Designers are the facilitators of this long-term process, and that is a huge responsibility.

Glossary

This glossary is a quick introduction for some of the commonly used terms in the book, including explanations on how they are handled. This is especially true for the term *MR* for mixed reality. The MR definition is often debated, as explained later on.

XR

Stands for extended reality and is the umbrella term for all variations of spatial computer interactions, including VR, AR, and MR. XR is often interchangeably used with immersive media or spatial computing.

VR

Virtual reality creates an artificial three-dimensional environment for interaction. Virtual reality is as unlimited as the human imagination and has been the subject of sci-fi pop culture, such as in Neal Stephenson's 1992 novel *Snow Crash* and Ernest Cline's 2011 novel *Ready Player One.*

AR

Augmented reality is an information layer over the existing physical world. AR is used with mobile phones or tablets as handheld AR or via headsets as AR headsets or glasses, to assist in a real-world context. AR typically uses cameras for environment tracking, to enable interaction with overlaid or embedded digital objects in the user's surrounding.

Immersive media

Covers all XR media, but could theoretically also include VR cave installations or noninteractive media as stereoscopic viewers and so on. It is typically used interchangeably with XR and spatial computing.

© Cornel Hillmann 2021
C. Hillmann, *UX for XR*, https://doi.org/10.1007/978-1-4842-7020-2

Spatial computing

Is the umbrella term for spatial interactions typically in an XR context. Spatial computing can also include technologies beyond XR, such as Internet of Things (IoT)–based transactions and infrastructure technology. It is often used interchangeably with XR.

MR

Mixed reality; can refer to a number of things:

1. MR can be used interchangeably with AR: Both are defined as the embedding of virtual objects in the user's real-world environment.

2. MR can describe the merging of the two technologies VR and AR on a device basis. It means that a VR headset with AR capabilities, such as allowing camera see-through for AR interactions, can be called an MR headset or an AR headset with VR capabilities, for example, by dimming the otherwise transparent glasses to fade out the surrounding real world in order to bring in a fully artificial environment, can as well be labeled as an MR HMD.

3. MR can describe the merging of the two technologies VR and AR on an application basis, when an application for a social XR space is shared between AR and VR devices.

4. MR, or Microsoft Mixed Reality, is also the brand name for all Microsoft headsets, including all AR and VR headsets using Microsoft's technology.

5. Mixed Reality is the name of a capture technique using a green screen and virtual cameras (e.g., with the Unreal engine).

The MR controversy and the use of the term *mixed reality* in this book

The most controversial use of the term *mixed reality* is as a definition of a distinct technology between VR and AR. It has become widespread on the Internet to label MR as an intermediate technology that has more capabilities than AR by being able to embed objects into the environment. This description distinguishes between AR as a projection-only method and MR as an embedded virtual object method. This definition can be considered misleading, as it is not in line with academic and technical papers on the subject, in which this distinction has never existed, at least not in its recent history.

The claim that the occlusion feature in AR, the feature that allows AR objects to appear to exist alongside or behind real-world objects, should not be considered an AR feature and instead be labeled an MR feature is unsubstantiated by the evidence of all recently documented AR history.

The confusion has its roots in a 1994 paper by Paul Milgram and Fumio Kishino that makes these differentiations, while AR development since the 1990s has absorbed all these definitions.

Occlusion has since then and undisputedly so, without any doubt, been an AR feature, and there is very little use to distinguish between nonocclusion–enabled AR and occlusion-enabled AR under the MR flag. It doesn't solve any problems; instead, it adds confusion to the term *AR* and uncertainty to the definition of MR, which is already burdened with overlapping definitions. For that reason, this book uses only the MR definitions 1–5 (as defined in the preceding paragraph) and ignores the widespread description of MR as a "better AR."

The best idea is to consider MR as a very open and flexible term that can be used interchangeably with XR (in the Microsoft definition) or interchangeably with AR as often used in consumer publications. The advantage of the term *mixed reality*: Consumers instantly understand what it means, sort of.

3DOF

Three degrees of freedom is the definition for an earlier generation of VR headsets, such as the Oculus Go, that only registered rotational movement without positional motion tracking. A 3DOF headset is, therefore, less engaging and doesn't allow room-scale spatial interaction. Despite its simplicity, developers have found numerous ways to overcome the limitations with imaginative gameplay interaction. 3DOF headsets are not very common anymore, but still have a reasonable use case for their simplicity and flexibility, for example, the fact that they can be used in complete darkness or movement-restricted situations, like on an airplane. They may have a comeback as an immersive media player in the future.

6DOF

Is the full six degrees of freedom interaction type that entails rotational data as well as positional data: three degrees (X,Y,Z) for rotation and three degrees (X,Y,Z) for position. It allows the user to reach out and grab an item using the controller position, to duck and hide in an online battle, and to give a realistic simulation of a controller-driven tennis racket motion.

Inside-out tracking

Is the preferred motion tracking method of mobile and standalone headsets. The headset tracks the motion of itself and the controllers. The Oculus Quest and the latest Windows VR headsets use inside-out tracking.

Outside-in tracking

Is set up by using base stations that emit timed infrared pulses to be picked up by headset and controllers for precision motion tracking. It was originally established by Valve with SteamVR and Lighthouse for the HTC Vive HMD and is still used today for the Valve Index HMD. Outside-in tracking is often used in larger VR arcades as it allows for additional motion-tracked accessories and full-body motion tracking.

Handheld AR (HAR)

Handheld AR platforms are AR applications that run on any mobile device's 2D screen using the camera to track virtual objects in the context of the environment. HAR can be considered immersive because its interaction radius and play space is the 360-degree spatial environment of the user.

UX design

User experience (UX) design is the human-first approach to product design, a term encompassing all aspects of the end user's interaction with a process, a service, or a product, including, visual design, interaction design, usability and information architecture.

Digital product design

Is for the most part identical as UX design, but it can entail areas that are not concerned with the user perspective, such as user data collection. The other theoretical difference from UX design is the equal balance of user experience to business goals. Very often, UX designers are hired as product designers.

Game design

Game design is identical to digital product design in its goals. It has an emphasis on entertainment software using different design methods. As it entails the same areas, including early research, concept prototyping, and testing, it is also used for non-entertainment products as a production approach, using the same production methods, tools, and principles established by game productions.

UX/UI design

Typically is focused on the visual and aesthetic side of UI interactions, including typography content and layout, color schemes, and branding. For web and mobile applications, it entails the entire visual experience, and for 3D interactive apps and games, it is focused primarily on menu interactions.

This book describes web and mobile design as the main areas of 2D UX design. Typically, this would also entail software UI design. However, as the majority of UX jobs are in web and mobile app design, this is the focus. The term *product design* is interchangeably used with UX design in this book, referring to the typical situations where UX designers are hired as product designers, even though UX design has slightly different priorities in theory and occasionally expresses a different mindset. The fact is that UX designers have always had to incorporate the business needs into the design. It has also become a trend in the industry to replace the term *UX design* with the term *product design* to express the larger sphere of its ambition and the reality of how it is used in practice. UX design and product design follow exactly the same design thinking process.

Resources

Oculus UX resources:

developer.oculus.com/learn/design-accessible-vr-ui-ux/

Microsoft MR design resources:

docs.microsoft.com/en-us/windows/mixed-reality/design/design

Tvori:

tvori.co

Advanced Framework for the Unreal engine:

humancodeable.org

VR Interaction Framework for Unity:

beardedninjagames.com/vr-framework

MRTK Unity:

docs.microsoft.com/en-us/windows/mixed-reality/mrtk-unity/

MRTK UX Tools for the Unreal engine:

microsoft.github.io/MixedReality-UXTools-Unreal/README.html

Object-Oriented UX:

objectorientedux.com

AltspaceVR:

altvr.com

Mozilla Hubs:

hubs.mozilla.com

Half-Life: Alyx:

half-life.com/en/alyx

Books:

Unreal for Mobile and Standalone VR: Create Professional VR Apps Without Coding by Cornel Hillmann (Apress, 2019)
apress.com/gp/book/9781484243596
The History of the Future by Blake J. Harris
harpercollins.com/products/the-history-of-the-future-blake-j-harris

Index

A

Adobe Aero, 58, 139, 143, 162–165

Advanced Framework (AF), 222, 223

AltspaceVR, 92, 182

Android Package (APK) file, 225

Animation, 56–58, 91, 99, 106, 139, 140

AR objects, 57, 140, 142–144, 168, 243

Artificial intelligence (AI), 21

Augmented reality (AR)

Ask Mercedes, 56

aspect, 63

computer vision, 51

device category, 53

environment situations, 52

gamification, 71, 72

idea, 61

location-based, 57

machine learning, 52

Magicverse, 61

marker-based, 56

messaging apps, 50

Microsoft HoloLens, 51

privacy UX, 60–63

projection-based, 54

remapping, 62

road map, 55, 56

sensor technology, 52

Snapchat, 57

types, 52, 53

UX design, 57–59

UX designers, 54

B

Battlefield Augmented Reality System (BARS), 20

Blockchain, 61, 75, 201, 203, 228

Brain-computer interface (BCI), 46, 145, 230

C

Classic storytelling principles, 198

Conventions, VR, 94, 95

affordances, 94

buttons, 96, 97, 101

change of, 104

comfort zones, 97

constant velocity, 100

curved screens, 95

diegetic elements, 96

hand interaction, 98, 99

Printed in Great Britain
by Amazon

75393439R00159